A Kierkegaard Handbook

Other books by Frederick Sontag

Divine Perfection: Possible Ideas of God
The Existentialist Prolegomena: To a Future Metaphysics
The Future of Theology: A Philosophical Basis for Contemporary Protestant
 Thought
The Problems of Metaphysics
The Crisis of Faith: A Protestant Witness in Rome
God, Why Did You Do That?
The God of Evil: An Argument from the Existence of the Devil
How Philosophy Shapes Theology: Problems in the Philosophy of Religion
The American Religious Experience: The Roots, Trends, and the Future of
 American Theology (with John Roth)
Love Beyond Pain: Mysticism Within Christianity
Sun Myung Moon and the Unification Church
God and America's Future (with John Roth)
What Can God Do?

A
Kierkegaard
HANDBOOK

FREDERICK SONTAG

Wipf and Stock Publishers
EUGENE, OREGON

Chapter 1 of this book is reprinted by permission from the pamphlet, slightly revised, published by the Press Department of the Ministry of Foreign Affairs of the Kingdom of Denmark, titled "Søren Kierkegaard: The Danish Philosopher," text by Peter P. Rohde.

The chapter, "Retrospective Summary," is reprinted with permission as revised from the author's Introduction to the Torchbook edition of Kierkegaard's *Authority and Revelation,* Harper & Row, New York, 1966. All page references in this section are to this edition.

Wipf and Stock Publishers
199 West 8th Avenue, Suite 3
Eugene, Oregon 97401

A Kierkegaard Handbook
By Sontag, Frederick
Copyright© January, 1979 Sontag, Frederick
ISBN: 1-59244-133-5
Publication date: January, 2003
Previously published by John Knox Press, January, 1979 .

For

B.B.

Teacher and Friend
Symbol of all those from whom I have learned,
Who for a quarter of a century urged that this
book be written

"You will learn the truth
And the truth will make you free."
John 8:32 (The Jerusalem Bible)

Preface

For many years this author has struggled to "understand Kierkegaard." Of course, that is what S.K. wanted his reader to do with him —struggle. This little book emerged as a result of that battle, but I do not assume that the outcome of reading it will be the same for everyone. In fact, given S.K.'s favorite category of "the individual," we should expect that every understanding, every solution, will be an individual one and will have to be made, finally, alone.

However, every beginning student of existentialism needs help. In this case, he needs a defense against S.K.'s tendency to overpower his reader with a torrent of unsorted and often confusing words. Yet, no matter how much we may want it, S.K. can never be explained to anyone in advance. No book is a substitute for submerging the would-be student in the maze of the Kierkegaardian massive literary production. Thus, this little text is not a summary or even a guide to S.K.'s thought. It cannot be, if S.K. was successful in his aim to force every reader to come to his or her own conclusion.

Yet, anyone who tries to understand Kierkegaard needs to know something of the man and his times as he begins this project. He also needs a conceptual scheme to use, so that he can begin to test his understanding of S.K. against some firm background. What this book proposes is that understanding Kierkegaard can best be done by mastering a handful of the key concepts which S.K. uses. Because he is intentionally an elusive author, the Kierkegaardian novice should try to understand these central concepts first as a base for reading S.K. himself.

This book does not then intend to stand alone. In fact, it cannot.

It is proposed only as a companion to reading Kierkegaard. It is only one point of reference, and the student can just as well turn to it after reading S.K. as before. That is, one might simply immerse himself in S.K.'s verbal flow, and then later resort to this book as a guide to help sort out the varied impressions.

Other terms and concepts not outlined here are crucial for understanding Kirkegaard. The reader is advised to keep notes of his own, a list of key concepts, as he makes his way through the Kierkegaardian corpus. S.K. has provided us with his own *Point of View* on his work as an author. That must be read and considered, too, as you make an overall appraisal. But by way of contrast, the reader is invited to test the Retrospective Summary which concludes the book as an alternative "point of view" on S.K.'s work as a whole. The next and final step, of course, is for the reader to produce his own perspective.

Since S.K.'s writings have no overall systematic plan, you may want first to read a little in a variety of his works and intersperse this with portions of the following chapters as a point of reference. This text is not meant to be read either first or all at one sitting. Once the reader has finished what he can cover of S.K.'s corpus, then reviewing these chapters which outline his major concepts may provide a way to collect your thoughts.

Each reader must work out his own appraisal or else miss Kierkegaard's central thrust as a philosopher. Thus, this introduction is not a substitute for individual thought but is an added stimulus to it. S.K. is confusing if he is anything, and he wants to be. One can not offer a "Kierkegaard made easy," but we can provide a way to approach S.K. so that his significance is not missed. In contrast to Kierkegaard's own personal and autobiographical *Point of View* on his work, this book is a systematic point of view. Its aim is to offer a net in which each reader can catch Kierkegaard—if he can.

My thanks go to the University of Copenhagen and to Professor Niels Thulstrop of the Kierkegaard Institute for the invitation to come to Copenhagen to lecture for a month in the fall of 1972. The core of this book was developed there. It was then expanded and revised over the next few years for use in mimeographed form in my classes on existentialism at Pomona College. Finally, Mrs. Gladys Burton typed the manuscript in its final form with great sensitivity.

—Frederick Sontag
Claremont, California

Contents

Søren Kierkegaard: The Man and His Times

Søren Kierkegaard was born in 1813, the year in which, as he says, "so many another bad note was put into circulation." This was the year of national bankruptcy after six years of a desperate and hopeless war with England as an ally of Napoleon. It marked the beginning of the poorest period in Danish history. S.K. died in 1855, two years before the abolition of the 400-year-old Sound dues, an action that introduced internal free trade. It marked the dismantling of the ramparts of old Copenhagen, along with the incorporation into the city of large new areas as sites for factories and working-class houses. Thus, 1857 was of all years the one in which the new age threw off the past and society began to be rapidly transformed by industrialism.

The old society, with its conservative and traditional outlook of the Guild System and Absolutism, was the social setting in which Kierkegaard lived and worked. In such an atmosphere a man can react in one of two ways: he can accept or he can rebel. Kierkegaard accepted and turned away from the affairs of this world. Yet, it is worth reflecting that he had a contemporary who deliberately chose the path of rebellion and whose posthumous renown has been even more brilliant than Kierkegaard's. This was Karl Marx. At exactly the same time as Marx and Engels were drafting their political programme, *The Communist Manifesto,* Kierkegaard was writing his religious manifesto in *The Works of Love.*

With all their dissimilarities, these two men have many points of resemblance. Both sprang from the same social situation and both reacted against the prevailing philosophy of Hegelianism, though in widely different ways. Marx sought to turn Hegelianism to account by, as he put it, "turning it upside down"—that is, right side up. Kierkegaard wanted to go much further and demolish the entire Hegelian system, on the ground that it is impossible to regiment the multiplicity of existence into a system. A system of thought is possible, but not a system of existence. This is the basic view which underlies all Kierkegaard's writings, and it has had a significant influence on modern philosophy through Existentialism.

Kierkegaard's life was outwardly uneventful. But to the ethical personality, it is not the number of events which matter but whether in experiencing them the individual allows his personality to be moulded by them. If he or she does, then the individual personality can make an indelible impression on those with whom he or she comes into contact. During his life Kierkegaard came into special contact with his father, the young woman to whom he became engaged, Regine, the poet and critic Meir Aaron Goldschmidt, and the bishops Mynster and Martensen.

A. The Father

Michael Pedersen Kierkegaard came from poor peasant stock in west Jutland. A grudging soil and a bleak climate produced a Puritan outlook still discernible in the local population today. In his childhood S.K.'s father tended sheep, but at a mature age he settled in Copenhagen as a wool merchant, and in time he amassed a considerable fortune. He also became a prominent figure in the city. Many of the intellectual elite of Copenhagen, headed by Bishop Mynster, would meet at his house. Though the wool merchant had received no education, by virtue of a vivid imagination and a penetrating intellect he was able to dispute with the scholars as though he were one of their own. But behind the old man's passion for arguing and philosophizing, there lurked the anxieties of a restlessly searching mind. Just as the son inherited his father's imagination and intellect, so, too, he was cradled in deep melancholy.

"There was a father and a son. Both intellectually very gifted, both witty—especially the father. Every visitor who knew their house found it, I think, very entertaining. Usually, they would only argue and converse together like two wits and not as father and son.

Occasionally, looking at the son and perceiving him to be greatly troubled, the father would stand in front of him and say: 'Poor child, you are living in a silent despair.' " This passage occurs in Kierkegaard's *Journals,* where he also says that his father made a perfect misery of his childhood. He realized early that there was a strange inconsistency between his father's piety and his inner unrest. There is an entry in the *Journals:* "The greatest danger is not when the father is a freethinker, or even when he is a hypocrite. No, the danger is when he is a pious and God-fearing man and when the child is intensely and profoundly convinced of this and yet feels that there is a deep disquiet in his soul, so that not even piety and godliness could give it peace. The danger lies precisely here, that the child in this situation is led to infer that God is not, after all, the God of infinite love."

In short, a suspicion crept in, corrupting the relationship between father and son and undermining the son's religious peace. One day the secret stands revealed. To quote from the *Journals:* "An affair between the father and son where the son finds everything out, and yet dare not admit it to himself. The father is a respectable man, God-fearing and strict; only once, when he is tipsy, he lets fall some words which arouse the most dreadful suspicions. Otherwise the son is never told of it and never dares to ask his father or anybody else."

What it was that the son in an unguarded moment had learnt we do not know for certain, but it is natural to suppose that it concerned a sexual offense. We know that the father married a servant in the house a year after his first wife's death and that the second wife (Søren's mother) gave birth to a son only two months after their marriage. It is certain that the revelation was a mental shock to the son which disturbed not only his faith in his father but his whole moral outlook. It threw him into a period of dissipation and despair, during which he completely neglected his theological studies at the University.

From his father he had acquired an Old Testament religiousness which never left him. In his father's despair he saw a judgment of God, in his wealth and prosperity a curse, and in his great age a warning that he was to outlive all his children, a view which was shared by the old man himself. However, the father died in 1838, and the event caused the son to pull himself together. He saw that he had been mistaken and felt under an obligation to redeem his promises to his father and pass his examination, now that he could no longer deceive the old man, as he said. He did so in the course of the next two years.

B. Regine

At the same time he became engaged to a sixteen-year-old girl of the Copenhagen bourgeoisie called Regine Olsen, whom he had known and felt attracted to for a year or more. However, the engagement was scarcely a fact before he began to have scruples. To quote the *Journals:* "The second day (after the engagement) I saw that I had blundered. A penitent as I was, my vita ante acta, my melancholy— that was enough." In other words, Kierkegaard felt that he could never conquer his melancholy. He was unable to confide in the young woman what he considered to be the causes of it. His father's figure blocked the way, and the tragedy of the family curse was something which could not be divulged. He was thrown in upon himself and his solitude, incapable of "realizing the universal." That is, he could not live in a mutual human relationship of confiding in or depending on others, or even of preaching or teaching for a living, an intention which he frequently considered but never carried out.

Two months later he had decided that he was not justified in binding the light-hearted young woman to him and by his melancholy making her, too, unhappy. On the other hand, to break off an engagement was in those days a serious matter and might place the woman in an unfavorable light. To save Regine, therefore, Kierkegaard resolved to take all the blame on himself, in a way that would make everybody believe it was she who had broken off the engagement. For several months he went through the comedy of posing as an irresponsible philanderer, noisily showing off in public, endeavoring to turn appearances against himself by every means in his power. He was partly successful; but the one person he failed to deceive was Regine, who saw through the ruse and refused to accept the breach. In consequence it was doubly distressing to both of them. When the break was an accomplished fact, Kierkegaard wrote in his *Journals:* "When the bond broke, my feeling was this: Either you plunge into wild dissipation, or into absolute religiousness—of a different kind from the parson's melange."

He chose the latter. But he also chose something else. He chose authorship. It was in November 1841 that he finally broke with Regine. A fortnight later he went to Berlin (the only foreign place he ever saw and which he visited twice) in order to escape from the scene of these harrowing experiences. There he began to write. It came over him like a torrent, driving him incessantly during the next ten years —the most concentrated period of production by any Danish author and surely one of the most compact in world literature. The real year of his debut was 1843. Before then he had written only a few occasional pamphlets and his University dissertation, *On the Concept of Irony with Constant Reference to Socrates.* But in 1843 he published no fewer than six books, the first being the biggest he ever wrote. Its significant title is *Either/Or,* and it takes us straight into the world of Kierkegaard's ideas.

An "either/or" confronts one with a choice, and in fact it is Kierkegaard's intention to force the reader to choose. We must choose how we wish to live our lives and not just passively drift down life's river. In *Either/Or* he presents the reader with two different ways of life which he calls the "aesthetic" and the "ethical." However, he attaches a different meaning to "aesthetic" from the one we normally associate with the word. He uses it to denote the immediate life of the senses which is the starting point of all human activity. In the first part of his work, he shows us a variety of aesthetic lives and types. These move from the lowest, which is sensual and nothing but sensual as represented in the figure of Don Juan, to the man who has experienced the emptiness of a purely aesthetic life but who nevertheless clings to it knowing that it leads only to despair.

Why does a life lived on the aesthetic plane lead only to despair? Because, according to Kierkegaard, man has in him something else which is not satisfied by a life of the senses. This something else is the eternal. Man, he says, is compounded of widely different and divergent elements. He is, declares Kierkegaard, a synthesis of body and spirit, temporal and eternal, finite and infinite, necessity and freedom. It is characteristic of the aesthetic, however, that it places all the emphasis on one side of the synthesis: the bodily, the temporal, the finite, the necessary. The other side is none the less present. It makes its presence felt as an anxiety, an uneasiness, "a sympathetic antipathy and an antipathetic sympathy," something at once frightening and attractive. The term which best describes this call of the spirit in the world of the senses, Kierkegaard discovers, is "dread" (angst). The experience of dread, then, is an indication that man has within him the eternal. Without the eternal and without an experience of emptiness, there would be no dread. But the man who has felt the dread within him, yet obstinately persists in an existence in the sphere of the senses, is doomed to despair. On these concepts, of dread and despair, Kierkegaard wrote two of his most brilliant books: *The Concept of Dread* (1844) and *The Sickness Unto Death* (1849).

Now, the man who has been made to realize the inadequacy of a life in the aesthetic sphere by the voice of dread, and who does not despairingly cling to it in spite of his realization, will mature enough to choose something else and enter the ethical sphere. This is a realm distinguished by the eternal having asserted its claims on the man. He then not only accepts it but also believes in the possibility of realizing the ethical demands in the temporal world of the senses.

But as in the aesthetic world, so also in the ethical. It is necessary to distinguish between various stages of development. At his lowest stage of development, a man still believes he is able to honor the claims of eternity in the temporal world. At his highest stage of development, the ethical man has learnt how little he is capable of by his own exertion. The man who attains this realization has reached the maturity to cross over from the ethical sphere and enter the "religious," which is based on this recognition of the inadequacy of human endeavor. Here we come to the end of *Either/Or*, and it may be said that the choice it offers the reader is really a "neither/nor": Neither the aesthetic nor the ethical is sufficient to enable man to realize the eternal life in the temporal world; only by entering the religious can this be done.

In the following years these ideas were elaborated in a number of other works, notably *Stages on Life's Way* (1845). The title is a variation of the *Either/Or* theme, only now the argument is further developed into the religious. In *Philosophical Fragments* (1844), Kierkegaard discusses the essential Christian problem of how the eternal can manifest itself in time, God and history. In *Concluding Unscientific Postscript* (1846), his main philosophical work, he once and for all disposes of philosophical systematization with its belief in the possibility of objective cognition. His polemics are directed at the faith in a scientific system implicit in Hegelianism, and he formulates the thesis that "subjectivity is truth." This does not imply that truth is relative, or that there is no such thing as absolute truth. It is intended to cut the ground from under the feet of those who think they can sit dispassionately and disinterestedly at their desks and reason their way to the truth about the ultimate problems of life. The truth can be found only by passionate search and by applying one's whole personality existentially. The criterion of the genuine search for truth is "inwardness" or an intense personal concern with it.

C. Goldschmidt

After completing this long series of pregnant works, Kierkegaard intended to stop writing and accept a living as a parson in a remote part of the country. But this was not to be. By this time he was an established and acclaimed author. One of his warmest admirers was the young poet and journalist Meir Aaron Goldschmidt, who at the age of 21 had started to publish a political journal, *The Corsair.* On the basis of Liberalism, it attacked the Absolutist regime, Conservatism, censorship, and anything that smacked of reaction. The editor's method was derisive satire, and few escaped his acid pen. One of the few was Kierkegaard, whose genius Goldschmidt clearly appreciated. Kierkegaard, for his part, inclined to the view that *The Corsair* was a gutter press. At length he came out with a newspaper article expressing his repugnance at receiving praise from a paper of this type and demanding abuse instead. Kierkegaard's intention with this letter was to confront Goldschmidt, whose talent he appreciated and of whom he entertained certain hopes, with a choice, an "either/or": Either he must reveal himself as the blackguard he might well have been, or he must think twice and abandon his scurrilous methods.

Goldschmidt's reply was immediate. True, there was no abuse, but in several issues of the paper he ridiculed Kierkegaard's person in text and in caricature. Caricature is nowadays an indispensable feature of newspapers, even the most respectable. In those days it was something new, and to the contemporary view it seemed the last word in caddishness. Kierkegaard was deeply stung. He saw himself a general laughing-stock, and it had a tremendous influence on him. It fanned the intellectual aristocrat's contempt of the common man that had always smouldered within him. Now his scorn for the masses flared up. The majority is always wrong, he states in his *Journals:* Truth is always in the minority. The minority is always stronger than the majority, because the minority is made up of those who really have an opinion. The strength of the majority is illusory, since it is formed by the rabble who have no opinion. "Nobody will be that exhausting thing, the individual. But everywhere they are at your service with the lying substitute, a few. Let us unite, be a few; then we shall be strong. This is the deepest demoralization of the human race."

In particular, his contempt and irony are directed at the clergy, who make themselves comfortable in secular society and follow the majority. Above all, he regards them as traitors to their appointed office. Gradually the idea ripens in his mind that the only man who can point the way forward is the one who is ready to lay down his life in martyrdom. And with this realization comes the question: What of himself in this connection? Is he the man called upon to lay down his life? Has God entrusted him with a special mission? A suspicion forms in his mind in these years that God may have chosen him to speak directly to his contemporaries. Is he to speak *with authority,* as the Apostles had done?

This idea matured only gradually and in the face of many doubts and scruples. For who can speak with authority? Who can presume to testify? Of course, only the man who can conform to the testimony. But no man can conform to the testimony of Christianity, for no man is without sin. Hence all his writings so far had deliberately avoided any form of testimony. He had never set out to convert men to Christianity. His whole endeavor had been concern with showing his contemporaries what Christianity really was, or should be, if it was to have any meaning. Running through all his work had been the "either/or" on which he had based his first book. You can be a Christian, or you can refuse to be a Christian: It is your own affair, and only you yourself can make the decision. But you shall not have the excuse for shirking the choice by saying that you were unaware of what Christianity was, what it was all about.

That had been the background to Kierkegaard's past authorship. It was no testimony; there was no preaching—only expounding. He had told his contemporaries what Christianity meant. And to emphasize the fact that he wrote without authority, he had published his works under various pseudonyms. None of them could be directly identified with Kierkegaard himself. In this way he aimed at the "midwifery" proclaimed by Socrates. He wanted to help people to choose by making them realize what their choice is all about. Yet nobody could make the choice for them. At the moment of choosing, a man is alone with himself and his responsibility.

Kierkegaard had strongly insisted that he preached no doctrine and that he spoke without authority. Thus the idea of coming forward and personally testifying seemed to him like a break with his whole past. No wonder we find him hesitating and uncertain. An event was necessary before he could venture to take the plunge into direct testimony.

D. Mynster-Martensen

The event which set things in motion was the death of Bishop Mynster. Mynster had been Bishop of Zealand and Primate of the Church of Denmark for twenty years. He had exerted a great influence on old Michael Pedersen Kierkegaard. Partly out of duty to his father, the son had continued to respect the great prelate. Above all else Mynster was a man of great culture and a man of the world. There is no reason to doubt his personal piety, but this was inseparable from his general culture. It drew its strength as much from the Classics and from Goethe as from the Gospels. We detect in Søren Kierkegaard, as time passes, a growing criticism of the aging bishop, whose form of Christianity seemed to him a falsification.

> Bishop Mynster's service to Christianity is really this, that by his outstanding personality, his culture, his superiority in fashionable circles, he developed the fashion or convention that Christianity was something which no deep-thinking and serious man, no person of culture, could dispense with. To an eternal and Christian view, however, this service seems rather ambiguous. For surely Christianity is a little too great to be patronized.

And in his earnestness there is some melange—so touched he is, so deeply moved, at the thought of its glories—and when it comes to the point so touchy about being ever so slightly belittled himself . . . and yet I love Bishop Mynster. My one desire is to do everything to enhance his prestige, for I have admired him, and as a man I admire him yet; and every time I can do something to his good I think of my father, whom I believe this pleases.

Thus wrote Kierkegaard in his *Journals* in 1848. Later the tone got sharper: "In the splendid Palace Chapel a stately Court preacher, the cultivated public's elite, advances before an elite circle of fashionable and cultivated people and preaches emotionally on the text of the Apostle, 'God chose the mean and despised'—and nobody laughs!" For his part Mynster had no great regard for Kierkegaard and kept him at arm's length, rightly suspecting a dangerous rebel in him. In spite of the latent opposition between the two men, Kierkegaard continued to show deep respect for Mynster as long as the latter lived. He felt that he owed this to his father's memory.

But in 1854 Mynster died and was succeeded by Martensen. Martensen was a man of some distinction. His *Christian Dogmatics* enjoyed a European reputation. He had made a study of Christian mysticism, notably in Jacob Bochme whose writings had opened up new perspectives. However, he was also an orthodox Hegelian with the self-imposed task of confuting the subjectivity of Romantic morals by "a theoretical knowledge of objectivity, of the concluded form of the state and religion, science and art." His theological writings were thus markedly speculative in character. They culminated in a dogma which systematized the Christian world of ideas right down to the order of precedence of the angels.

For such a man Kierkegaard could have no sympathy. In his funeral oration over Bishop Mynster, Martensen went so far as to call him "one of the witnesses for the truth who, like a sacred chain, stretch down the ages from the days of the Apostles." Thereby, in a sense, he elevated the admired and idolized Mynster to the ranks of the martyrs. Kierkegaard could restrain himself no longer. This seemed to him to be blasphemy and a corruption of all Christian values. There had to be a protest.

This was the starting point for the last phase of Kierkegaard's authorship. He abandoned pseudonymity, and in a series of pamphlets he addressed himself to the public directly. He did this in order to open its eyes to the falsification of Christianity which was being carried out by the clergy in the name of Christianity. The attacks culminated in the publication of the little journal called *The Instant,* which appeared in nine issues. The tenth was ready for publication when Kierkegaard collapsed in the street and had to be taken to the hospital. He died shortly thereafter, shattered by the prodigious internal strain imposed by his struggle against the Established Church.

Kierkegaard's attack on official Christianity had wide repercussions in Denmark and permanently influenced the Danish Church. It has become less institutional than, perhaps, any other Church in the world. Yet it is not the attack on the Church which first springs to mind when we look for the causes of Kierkegaard's influence today. However justified the onslaught may have been, it was rather extravagant, conditioned as it was by a craving for individualism, asceticism, and resignation. The last entries in his Journals, written a few days before he broke down, begin with these words: "The purpose of this life is—to be brought to the highest pitch of world-weariness." His life had led him from quiet resignation, engendered by his engagement to Regine, to a consistent denial of all affirmation in life. The clash with Goldschmidt had intensified his pessimistic view of man, and the conflict with the Church had made him despair of getting even the clergy to live by the Christian message. But this abnegation of the world only gradually entered into his writings, and it does not color the works which he wrote before launching his assault.

What sustained the interest in Kierkegaard and gave him international importance before and since the war is something totally different: It is the battle he waged on philosophical systematization, with its belief that the riddles of existence can be solved by speculative means. He made it an absolute demand that ideas should be translated into existence. This, in his opinion, is exactly what the contemporary philosophers failed to do: "Most systematizers stand in the same relation to their systems as the man who builds a great castle and lives in an adjoining barn; they do not live in their great systematic structure. But in spiritual matters this will always be a crucial objection.

Metaphorically speaking, a man's ideas must be the building he lives in—otherwise there is something wrong."

It was, of course, especially Hegel—the systematizer par excellence—against whom Kierkegaard aimed his shafts. He admired Hegel's intellectual capacity but declared that his system could give nobody the key to existence: "If after writing his whole *Logic* Hegel had said in the Preface that it was only an intellectual exercise (and that at many points he had even shirked things), he might have been the greatest thinker that has ever lived. Now he is a comic." Hegel had never grasped the simple fact that it is impossible to understand existence intellectually. "It is quite true what philosophy says, that life must be understood backwards; a thesis which, the more we reflect on it, leads precisely to the conclusion that life in the temporal world never becomes properly understandable, for the very reason that at no moment of time can I find the perfect repose to take up the backward position."

This appreciation of the limited range of the intellect, and its powerlessness to deal with the ultimate problems of life, increasingly permeated the philosophy of the twentieth century. This has split philosophy into a pure science pursuing limited objectives and a moral philosophy of life which discusses the ultimate problems of existence while making no claims to the title of science in the strict sense of the word. It has found its most characteristic formulation in Existentialism, which influenced philosophical thought both in Germany and in France. It has spread to the Anglo-Saxon world and also has enthusiastic disciples in Italy and Spain. Kierkegaard is the progenitor of all Existentialist thinkers. He was the first in modern times who strove deliberately to think existentially. That is, he was fully conscious that we understand backwards but live forwards: Thus, when we direct the light of knowledge on the problems of existence, we do it neither dispassionately nor disinterestedly, but with the application of our whole personality.

Curiously enough, Denmark had two great religious figures at the same time. Both in various ways made a point of thinking existentially. Besides Kierkegaard there was Grundtvig. They differed immensely in almost everything: Indeed they were the two poles of Danish thought in the nineteenth century. Kierkegaard was the supreme individualist, bent on isolating the individual with his responsibility. Grundtvig emphasized fellowship in all its forms, and so became a major force in Danish national life. Yet they agreed on one thing: Both opposed systematic philosophy and speculative systematization. Both resisted the idea that the antitheses of existence could be made to vanish into a higher synthesis. They did not want to rob life of its tension or the Christian view of existence of its meaning as a struggle between good and evil.

Each in his way has meant a great deal to the intellectual life of Denmark. Measured by an international standard, Kierkegaard must come first. Grundtvig expressed his view of life in his poetry, which is untranslatable in its individual style and its obscure symbolism. Kierkegaard employed a crystal-clear dialectic which can easily be transplanted into other languages, even though much is lost because he is also a great literary artist with a rare sense of style. Still, there is always enough left so that the meaning of what he wrote will never be in doubt. Using the weapons of logic and philosophy, he performed the feat of demonstrating the impotence of logic and philosophy to deal with the ultimate problems of existence. This demonstration is his real title to fame. It was not meant to belittle logic and philosophy but to make it difficult for us to abuse these instruments to obtain fictitious solutions to problems they are powerless to solve.

Aesthetic/Ethical

If we must grasp the meaning of certain terms in order to gain an understanding of Kierkegaard, aesthetic (or esthetic) is most certainly one of these. In the first place, it is not possible to understand what "existentialism" means without seeing it in contrast to the aesthetic life, and the same is true of S.K.'s view of Christianity. Furthermore, it is not possible to understand the struggle going on within S.K.'s own life, and the reflection of this in his writing, without recognizing the aesthetic qualities in his personal mode of existence and his own fight against this.

Aesthetic means "distance from reality." That is, one transforms life poetically so as to remove its element of sorrow and replace it with pleasure. The aesthetic component in life is important, and it ought not to be removed hastily in some burst of zeal. It is only after happiness has been exploited that the moral and the religious qualities are able to appear by way of contrast (Hong & Hong: *Journals & Papers,* p. I-368). What is aesthetic is also connected to the important notion of "repetition," since it is the aesthetic quality that allows an experience to be repeated without growing dull *(ibid.).*

S.K. constantly contrasts the aesthetic love of beauty with the Christian life, so that Christianity must also be understood as the fight against the dominance of aesthetic pleasure. A poet must be unhappy in his heart, but his aesthetic gift enables him to transform this into a form of joy in his work as an author. The pleasure produced by the poet's imagination helps to induce repetition, because his work can satiate us many times over, much more so than any real-life pleasure.

The aesthetic tendency in the reader makes him admire an idea rather than believe in the actuality behind it. Thus, the idea is far less dangerous than the existence it comes from (*ibid.,* p. I-371). The aesthetic tendency can, therefore, stand as a barrier to commitment in faith, although it is also true that religious faith is not understandable except in contrast to aesthetic neutrality. Beauty is the norm of aesthetic enjoyment, but to transform the whole of religious life in this way is to destroy it.

Aesthetic presentation always creates a distance between the person and reality (*ibid.,* p. I-370), whereas the goal of life is to be immediately involved in the concrete situation. Poetically, we present ideas which are aesthetically attractive, but this is very different from striving after an ideal in fact. The goal of the poet is to hold the matter at a distance and to produce pleasure thereby. The medium of imagination works to take us away from the terrifying actuality of real people (*ibid.,* p. I-374). The poetic presentation charms us; actuality makes us flee. For this reason "aesthetic" is also associated with "possibility," since it is opposed to actuality too.

The poet, or the erector of the aesthetic life, lives in possibility rather than actuality. Artistic polish removes us from life because it deals in possibilities and enables us to live in that pretense. Art both creates a detached moment and enables us to live in it. Religion requires action, which is opposed to the aesthetic tendency to enjoy the moment. Religious ceremony is more aesthetic than real, since life outside churches does not proceed very ceremoniously.

When S.K. presents the aesthetic life to us in *Either/Or* (trans. Lowrie, Princeton: Princeton University Press, 2 Vols., 1944) the "papers of A" contained in Volume I reveal the purely aesthetic life in contrast to the ethical. Yet, although S.K. describes the aesthetic life in its fullness, particularly in "The Rotation Method," in his humorous and ironical preface he himself suggests that both sets of papers might be viewed as the work of one man.

This remark should serve to remind us that the aesthetic and the ethical—also the religious—are not separate but actually are bound together in one man. If the inner life is not the outer appearance, as S.K. suggests (p. 3), a man might live an aesthetic existence outwardly and still be ethical in his inward grasp of himself—at least in part. If the ear is the organ for the apprehension of inwardness, the eye provides us with the constant paradox of an aesthetic surface spread out before us which does not fit what we hear about the inner life.

Of course, our ethical sense makes us struggle to bring the external mode of existence into correspondence with its inner condition. Seriousness fights a constant battle with the gloss of an aesthetic surface. The aesthetic man attempts to avoid contradiction, but the ethical man is doomed to a continual battle with the transforming qualities of the aesthetic imagination that does not allow reality a direct expression. "Chance" is crucial to the aesthetic life, and one cannot remove this simply by an attempt at systematic understanding. In the strictest sense, the aesthetic life can be appreciated but it can never be fully understood.

The poetic mood dominates whatever is aesthetic (p. 8), so that the poet's art is the prime example of the transforming quality which the aesthetic approach involves. Yet such an enterprise cannot be consistent and coherent; to be so would be a contradiction in terms. The "Diapsalmata," which is the first of A's papers, reflects the quality of the discontinuous, of momentary sayings. The opening lines describe the poet and indicate that he must first experience suffering in his heart, which he then transforms into something of beauty. Therefore, the aesthetic life cannot be pure joy, as is sometimes supposed. It needs an intimate connection with inner suffering as the source of its drive to transform existence aesthetically. "Melancholy," perhaps S.K.'s favorite state, is also involved in the drive toward creativity. The aesthetic surface is smooth, but its interior origins are not.

In the aesthetic mood S.K. also praises "passion." It is first thought of as the needed drive toward the ethical life, but passion also appears to be equally necessary as an ingredient in any creative effort. "The Ancient Tragical Motive," for instance, belongs in A's aesthetical papers, although tragedy seems far from the aesthetic. "Just as weeping is natural to all men alike" (p. 113), so sorrow is a part of aesthetic inspiration, even though the aim of aesthetic existence is to clothe sorrow in a pleasing form. In order to be aesthetic, creative results must remain essentially open and unfinished. The poetic personality never completes or summarizes its work (p. 124). S.K.'s

"Shadowgraphs" derive from the darker side of life, but the form of expression used keeps this from becoming fully visible. Its origins are necessarily incompletely disclosed.

"Life does not obey esthetic norms" (p. 149), and thus the poetic always moves away from reality into a world of its own making. However, the presence of S.K.'s short essay on "The Unhappiest Man" in the midst of this volume creates a problem for any simple interpretation of the aesthetic life. This analysis of unhappiness is a part of A's papers, and yet it surely reflects reality. "Emptiness" is its theme, whereas the aim of the aesthetic impulse is to keep life constantly full. If the unhappy man is said to have the fullness of his existence outside himself (p. 181), we can conclude that the aim of the aesthetic man should be to have the content of his life present in every moment. Yet the production of an aesthetic effect depends on the interruption of the accidental. This ties success in the aesthetic life to our ability to deal constantly with the accidental in a skilled and novel way.

Thus, S.K.'s essay on "The Rotation Method" begins by noting the latent creative power present in boredom, which indicates how delicate the balance is between the aesthetic life and its opposite. In using the rotation method, one becomes inventive by limiting himself. This indicates the control which is necessary if you are to be successful in creating the aesthetic life. It cannot be lived casually, and yet at the same time it must not fall into the trap of seriousness. "Forgetting" is an art, and it lies at the center of aesthetic skill, for one may venture and yet not be hurt if he has perfected the art of forgetting at will. "Arbitrariness" (p. 245) is the secret of such a life, for such skill in manipulation prevents you from being tied to seriousness or reality and to the demands of the ethical. Let the arbitrary in you correspond to the accidental in the world, we are advised.

The section on "The Diary of the Seducer" is an example of S.K.'s aesthetic attempt to weave a little gloss around existence. The task of living poetically is to intrude the poetic personality into experience so that it becomes impossible "to distinguish poetry and reality from one another" (p. 253). The poetic thus becomes present in the ambiguity of life. The poetic personality has much to do with reality, but the trick is that he does not allow himself to be captured by it. The aesthetic man lives entirely intellectually and thus his seductions are mostly mental. He holds himself away from reality. However, the reader can also find the aesthetic present in the second volume, that is, in the ethical writings. S.K.'s essay on "The Esthetic Validity of Marriage" can only be understood as a protest after we have mastered the secret of living aesthetically.

The man who lives in a constant aesthetic-intellectual intoxication is a danger to the man who expects to be dealt with on a purely intellectual level. Romantic life is immediate, as all aesthetic life is, but marriage adds an ethical and religious dimension to this which is an unwilling burden for the aesthetic personality. Freedom and necessity are brought together in the marriage vow, but the aesthetic man attempts to keep freedom unrestricted. However, if we were ever tempted to think that S.K. preferred the too-simple solution of accepting either the aesthetic or the ethical life to the exclusion of the other, his essay on "Equilibrium" may offer us the key to his real conclusion. He tells us that the ethical and aesthetical must be balanced in the composition of personality. This is very different from talking about the aesthetic as a deception to be purged entirely in some dramatic attempt to face reality directly.

The "Either/Or" in our choice between an aesthetic or an ethical way of life is demanded of us on some occasions, it is true. Nevertheless, the sensitive personality will attempt to keep both in equilibrium while still responding to the demand that he make a choice. The instant of choice is like the aesthetic moment (p. II-138), but the one requires skill in enjoyment and the other timely decisiveness. Without decisiveness life drifts on. The ethical man deplores aimlessness; the aesthetical man strives to enjoy it.

An aesthetic choice lacks ethical conviction and decisiveness, and therefore it is always capable of being retracted (p. II-141). To choose "merely aesthetically" is to choose without energy and pathos. It leaves the personality uninvolved and thus unchanged by the choice. The aesthetical is not evil, but neutrality is (p. II-143). A mental decision can be reversed too easily. The aesthetical in man is that whereby he is immediately what he is (p. II-150). He ignores the future and the decisions it demands. Instead, he is content with the present moment and any remaining pleasant memories of the past. Of course, it requires great intellectual gifts to live aesthetically. It can be done no more easily than the life of ethical decisiveness.

In fact, the aesthetic life may require greater skill and ability. The aesthete is the man from whom we learn how to enjoy life, but he will always shun a serious effort to understand life because it is disruptive of the moment. The immediacy of the child must be preserved in adulthood. Nevertheless, S.K. will assert later that the one who lives in immediacy is in despair whether he knows it or not (p. II-162). Beneath the surface, we need the intensity of despair, or the fear of falling into it openly. It provides the source of the strength required to live the aesthetic life of momentary enjoyment, as *Sickness Unto Death* will explain in detail. He who lives aesthetically seeks, therefore, as much as possible to live in a mood in such a way that the whole personality can be reflected in that mood without remainder. "He who lives esthetically sees only possibilities everywhere" (p. II-211). However, in his *Postscript,* S.K. returns to refine and review his statements on the aesthetic which serve as a way to define what is specifically "religious." In that sense, it is impossible ever to get rid of the aesthetic life entirely if we wish to understand what lies beyond it. Without it life would be devoid of contrast and equally lost in seriousness.

The difficult thing for Christianity to do is to wish for eternal happiness but not to confuse this with the aesthetic life. "Fortune, misfortune, fate, immediate enthusiasm, despair—these are the categories at the disposal of an esthetic view of life" (*Concluding Unscientific Postscript,* trans. David Swenson, Princeton University Press, 1944, p. 388). "There are thus three spheres of existence: the aesthetic, the ethical, the religious" (p. 448). But it is not clear that it is S.K.'s intention ever to say that the aesthetic can be fully overcome or surpassed. After all, his main thesis in his *The Point of View* is that he remained aesthetically productive until the end and was religiously active from the beginning.

In *The Point of View* (trans. Walter Lowrie, London: Oxford University Press, 1939), S.K. tries to tell us that he is and was a religious author whose aesthetic writings were a "deceit" in the service of Christianity (p. 6). Without analyzing fully this complicated self-evaluation, it is important for our understanding of "aesthetic" to point out that all aesthetic productions are "deceitful." They do not, they can not, intend to represent reality as it is. However, the most important point to note is that, as a writer, it is impossible not to be aesthetic if you use a written mode of communication. Words are never the way one comes into direct contact with reality. They are an aesthetic medium and are falsely used if one thinks they can in themselves reveal reality.

A duplicity is inevitable in all authorship, then. This is particularly true where the religious aspect is concerned, since a life lived on that plane can never be exhausted in words. Furthermore, all men naturally live part of their lives in aesthetic categories and so must be approached in this way. Can there be such a thing as a simultaneous aesthetic and religious production? That is the tension the religious author lives with, since he can never get rid of the aesthetic (p. 31).

The aesthetic work does involve a deception, but it is only permanent if one takes it as a more serious representation of reality than it is (p. 39). One can, after all, be deceived for truth's sake. Thus, when S.K. seems to speak as if he were rejecting and renouncing an aesthetic mode of communication altogether, it is important to look back at what he has said earlier and realize that it is impossible for man to stay alive and escape all aesthetic forms. They offer us the enjoyment of life and so constitute a constant challenge to all reality seekers.

We know that S.K. is interested in the "aesthetic" from his earliest written ventures. The topic is prominent in his *Journals,* and he comments on it in his earliest written work, his master's essay, *The Concept of Irony* (trans. Lee M. Capel, New York: Harper & Row, 1965). The aesthetic is again on his mind at the end of his life. His late work, *The Attack Upon Christendom,* can be viewed as a violent outburst which attempts, by its fury, to purge Christianity of its aesthetic gloss and to mature it in the reality of suffering. S.K.'s stress upon the martyr as the only true witness to the truth of Christianity can be accepted as his decision, reached in frustration, that martyrdom is the only way the aesthetic, i.e., the natural, approach to religion can be broken.

Repetition presents itself as that which the aesthetic man fears, because it forces him to face the reality of life by bringing it constantly around again. In fact, the aesthetic aim can be seen as an attempt to prevent the boredom which repetition involves through a constant use of inventive novelty. And the escape from repetition is critical for the aesthetic man, since, if unchecked, boredom opens us to the experience of dread. *The Concept of Dread* tells us that dread comes if one cannot sustain himself above emptiness and becomes dizzy and falls. Wherever we turn in S.K.'s writings, the "aesthetic" is crucial. This is true whether it is taken as that which we promote through increased skill in an effort to soften reality, or whether the aesthetic is that from which we constantly seek to escape into reality and religious commitment.

"The ethical," then, is Kierkegaard's contrasting concept to "the aesthetic," and it is necessary to understand both together. In that sense at least the aesthetic is never disposed of. Life ought not to be lived neutrally—this is S.K.'s chief message in stressing the ethical. We escape from the present world and its demands on us to decide by turning back in melancholy to childhood. Passion is the main thing one needs to break the spell and live decisively in the present. But "the ethical" does not simply mean facing reality. It involves bringing ideality (the world as it ought to be) in relation to reality. Doubt actually helps us, because it forces the individual to assume responsibility for the act or decision, which is the chief ingredient of the ethical life.

The highest life is not the philosopher's one of conceptualization. The best life needs to be resolved in action, which is the source of individual life. Yet to face ethical problems ought to induce anxiety and trembling, but it does not. We protect ourselves, cover ourselves with an aesthetic gloss. The highest expression of the ethical life is repentance, but that is painful, and we isolate ourselves from that by immediate enjoyment. To make health the highest good is an animal characteristic. The ethical demands more of man and so involves suffering. Affected virtue is in actuality a sin, since it takes the ethical life to be the easy way. Everything is full of significance in life, and nothing is indifferent if we grasp its ethical significance. Ethical consciousness alone is decisive in life. What one must not do is to postpone the decisive moment of life until what is to be decided is past.

The Christian must bring the eternal and the temporal together —that is his ethical task. And yet the highest life is to forsake or to give up the worldly. "Obedience" is a key concept too, if one wants to understand Christianity and the ethical. Yet Kierkegaard thinks the truly ethical individual makes himself so exceptional that he cannot be honored while he lives. Decision and resolution open up the best powers of the soul, but they also tend to alienate one from society. Suffering comes naturally to one who holds on to an ideal. Evil, in contrast, has a certain robust strength in the world. To live in the realm of the ethical means to be obligated, which restricts what one can do. Lecturing is easy. Ethical reduplication requires action and thus sacrifice. Ethically speaking, the task is ultimately to die to the world in order to see God.

Authorship/Corrective

As befits S.K.'s interpretation of his own work, it is possible to view his writings from many perspectives. One important way to do so is to claim that the aim of his whole literary authorship, and its guiding light, is to provide a "corrective" to the religious, theological and philosophical situation. Of course, his words can also be viewed as intended only for his time and for the situation he confronted in Denmark. However, on his own interpretation, a corrective is something which must be applied anew in every time and place. Thus, we must be careful to distinguish the particular correctives S.K. felt he must supply, that is, the ones he designed for his provincial circumstances, from the larger issue of corrective as a continued need. How is corrective to be applied, and why is it needed? What are its aims and intentions, and how can any "authorship" provide these?

S.K. tells us that "supplying the corrective" is essentially the task of "resignation" (Hong & Hong, *J & P,* p. I-331). If we consider this notion in the setting of the "knight of faith," we can see why he says this. That is, in the religious situation (see *Fear and Trembling*) one places himself against the universal and the ethical norm of society and so stands alone. Thus, the author who applies any corrective places himself outside the glad fellowship of the acceptable ways, and in doing so he must resign all hope for popular or public approval. A corrective is needed because what once was radical (e.g., Luther) now has become standard and thus is a road block to insight. All the favors the establishment can grant must be resigned by the author who undertakes the burden of once again supplying a corrective to his fellowmen. You cannot expect to enjoy the rewards of society and correct it at the same time.

Of course, once a corrective has been introduced and its need at least partially recognized, others will join and pretend that they themselves initiated it *(ibid.)*. It is the first spokesman who has the thankless job, and S.K. clearly thought of this as "my task." In a sense, part of the notion of what "existentialism" means develops from this, because he calls it an "existential-corrective" *(ibid.)*. In theory, in words and in institutions, we can think that things go on in life in the way in which we talk about them. The words which describe Luther's own reformation, and the corrective he applied, stand in contrast to the real situation S.K. saw as existing in the Danish state church. Thus, *corrective* is *existential* in that it attempts to turn us away from the maze of words and thoughts. The author's aim is to force us to see exactly how things are as lived out in the present. But what is a corrective at one time may become a deception later on.

A corrective can be poetically presented, as S.K. suggests. Aesthetics may seem far from the rough aim of corrective, whose goal is similar to radical reformation. But as S.K. explains to us in writing his *Point of View,* the author must find a way of getting the public's attention and putting his point across before he has any chance of being heard. Your aim as an author is to incite the people about the established order, but you must first present the ideals you want to be realized in a suitable poetic manner. The problem of how to gain attention is critical, for if the public were aware of what needed correcting, the corrective would not be required. Thus, any corrective must have popular appeal as well as technical power, although the trick is not to lose the sting in the aesthetic gloss of the medium the author employs.

Yet, every leader wants followers, and one source of confusion stems from the impatient leader who tries to readjust his corrective message to make it normative for others just so that he can gain approval. However, the very notion of corrective implies that it is not recognized as the norm at the time. To turn the reform into a popular cause confuses the corrective, because, if it is to have its effect, it must stand against any crowd.

However, there is no single fixed norm the author can follow, since what was a corrective in one generation will need to be opposed in another. Here S.K. yields to Hegel, as he sometimes does, and declares this relation to be "dialectical" (*ibid.,* p. 330). However, it is a dialectic without final resolution. It simply presents a continuous need and thus stands without Hegel's final synthesis. The problem is made more difficult because the relationship, once it is established, does not hold still. Luther's emphasis on grace was a corrective in his time (*ibid.,* p. 333), but it becomes confusing to another generation because they exhibit the opposite characteristics from the original situation. In a later time the earlier reform has become normative and so no longer can act as a corrective.

S.K. saw himself as the prophet of the "inner reformation," just as Luther had been the prophet of outward ecclesiastical reform. This is not because S.K. thought Luther saw everything religious solely in external terms. Not at all. But in due time, the inner reforms of Luther became merely outer rituals. S.K. hoped that his corrective might at least show us that inner reform is a constantly renewing need. Of course, the single work which stands out as the prime example of S.K.'s corrective is his *Attack on Christendom.* However, this book is no more than an overt and public example of what all of S.K.'s authorship aims to do to one degree or another. "Existentialism" for him means to force the decision back on each individual, not to allow anyone to borrow an important life-decision without first putting out his or her own effort.

Even S.K.'s edifying discourses aim to produce a change in the inner situation. They stand against—are a corrective for—a too easy or too placid notion of what the religious life involves. Since all life, and religious life par excellence, involves struggle, corrective is a constant necessity if we are to prevent the human tendency simply to collapse into acceptance. However, just as he saw his aesthetic works as a way to relate to the public, or just as he kept up regular church attendance throughout his life in spite of his *Attack,* so anyone who wants to be effective in correcting the establishment must get to know it and its weaknesses. Ironically, he must be related to or be a part of that which he would oppose.

Any corrective offered must be one-sided, since it aims to supply a missing aspect. Thus, it is easy to reject a reform as being "exaggerated," a description which indeed is true of much of what S.K. writes. The corrective must appear as an exaggeration, and therefore it can easily be misunderstood or rejected by anyone who wants to undercut it. In order to accomplish its task, the corrective must be as strong as possible, but such a lack of balance makes it easy for the establishment to ignore its reproof. A corrective cannot correspond to reality. It must be more severe than the facts warrant to be effective against the real situation. Therefore, any correction or reformation is open to rejection by anyone who takes reality as his standard of truth and assumes the desirability of moderation. The corrective will be upsetting and will appear to be an unnecessary commotion.

S.K. speaks out against the designation given to Bishop Mynster as a "witness to the truth." Given the setting of the speech as a funeral oration for a respected citizen and trusted friend, this reaction of S.K.'s in his *Attack* seems extreme and inappropriate to the situation. And it is, when viewed in that light, but the notion of what it means to be a Christian needed correction, in S.K.'s view. Only an exaggerated, a one-sided attack, could hope to dislodge a complacent notion. But any corrective will always appear "out of place" and "highly inappropriate" in the present situation.

S.K. wanted the reader to view his whole life and authorship as a corrective. S.K.'s broken engagement to Regine was a necessary corrective to his impulse toward happiness, which he felt had to be balanced both by his melancholy and by his commitment to an inner life. S.K. might have led both lives at once, but the broken engagement stood for him as a symbolic balance against any attempt to let the outer life gain dominance. His constant talk of becoming a country parson, on the other hand, stands as a corrective against his tendency to live an entirely interior existence. This cannot be interpreted as Hegel's dialectical movement, for there is no cumulative motion. The aim is to hold steady constantly at the beginning—where all men start. Thus, Kierkegaard never becomes a country parson, but he also never stops contrasting that role to his present life as a solitary writer.

"The Book on Adler" (*Authority and Revelation,* trans. Walter Lowrie, Princeton University Press, 1955) in a sense is S.K.'s own corrective against himself, just as *Attack* was a public corrective on the state of the church. That is, Magister Adler sought out S.K., thinking that because of S.K.'s stress on "subjectivity" he would support Adler's claim to have received a special revelation. Adler was under censorship by his church for these claims, but his plight became useful to S.K., so S.K. tells us. Adler pointed out certain things by his near insanity. In his book on Adler, S.K. gives us his best account of genuine authorship and its responsibility both to the Christian tradition and the health of its readers. Thus, Adler served as a corrective for S.K. too. Only an extreme position coming from outside could force S.K. to a deeper insight than he might have come to without this outside intrusion. It is this role which S.K. sought to play in the life of others.

"Inwardness," which S.K. took it as his mission to stress, also needs a constant corrective. It cannot be true inwardness unless it contains a challenge against every drift toward conformity to external norms. We sometimes think of inwardness as the needed corrective which S.K. wanted to provide for his age. Yet it is equally true that S.K. both needed something to correct him away from happiness (his resignation of marriage) and then again something to correct any tendency toward unrelated inwardness. This can be done by responding to a challenge, e.g., the Adler case. Renewal takes place by supplying the needed corrective to the challenge, in this case against authority, all of which brings inwardness into the spotlight of public attention.

"Dread" (see *The Concept of Dread*, trans. Walter Lowrie, Princeton University Press, 1946) is one of S.K.'s more famous correctives. Happiness can conceal the existence of dread and even its effects, and then innocence hides in the ignorance of what one must know (p. 37). Therefore, the task of the author is to give sinfulness a contemporary expression and hope thereby to bring to light the dread which all must face. There is no other way of restoring a man from his fall. Ignorance produces a state of innocence, but the overcoming of ignorance, which forces men to become aware of their condition, is the author's main task and his function as a corrective. He does not change men, but he can cause them to see their condition. Without the supplied corrective, they might remain unaware.

Language, unfortunately, also serves to conceal (p. 96), so that a frontal attack of words often cannot function as the needed corrective force. Again we come back to the notion that the corrective must be more severe than reality demands and not mild. S.K.'s outrage against Adler and Mynster are extreme, given the situation. Corrective is associated with the notion of being made aware that truth involves a form of deceit. That is, one must be deceived into the truth. He does not move into it naturally or willingly, at least where religious truth is concerned. The mild sermon is no sermon. "Paradox" in a real sense becomes the ultimate corrective, because it involves what is most difficult. It takes a strong push to shove men into truth, but that is the author's hard task.

The Concluding Unscientific Postscript defines truth as inwardness, as "subjectivity" (trans. David Swenson & Walter Lowrie, Princeton University Press, 1944; see Chapter II). This is intended as a corrective against the too easy assumption that one is formally a Christian. However, we should never forget that the historical and objective problems of Christianity must exist first before there can be a subjective issue. Ironically, the questions of historical fact must remain as a corrective against a too subjective treatment of Christianity. It is easy to repeat S.K.'s popular phrase that "objectively, Christianity has absolutely no existence" (p. 116), but this is too extreme and even misleading if it is accepted as a literal truth. It is meant as a corrective and so it must be overstated. It is better to risk being misunderstood than to avoid using the corrective power of an extreme.

This raises the whole problem of the way in which deception and being misunderstood are involved in the notion of corrective authorship. No one can serve as a corrective who does not risk the misunderstanding that comes due to the immoderate tone of his position. If you make yourself easily understood, this does not force on your reader his task of personal understanding. Somewhat paradoxically, only by first falling into misunderstanding or into an extreme position can the individual hope to correct himself into the truth. The external corrective of overstatement can be supplied by S.K. or another author, but the individual reader alone can add the next corrective that brings him to the truth.

It could be reasonably argued that in *Either/Or* (trans. David and Lillian Swenson, London: Oxford University Press, 1946, 2 Vols.)

S.K. first developed or made explicit the notion of the task of his authorship as a corrective. It is here that the ethical life is opposed to aesthetic enjoyment in "the Rotation Method." This involves urging an ethical commitment upon the devotees of pleasure in such a way that it serves as a corrective to their otherwise unrestrained enjoyment. To accomplish this the tone and form of personal writing are involved. The urgent appeal of a letter or the religious confrontation of the sermon suits the ethical mood. The variety of writing styles which S.K. employs, e.g., edifying discourse for the religious, are necessary if his words are to achieve their corrective intent.

Fear and Trembling is so obvious an example of corrective writing that it hardly needs to be elaborated. The easy way to religious faith must be blocked and confronted by a paradox. It is beside the point to discuss whether faith really does involve absolute isolation and demands that we embrace the absurd against reason. The point is that no corrective can be provided to an easy faith without developing a harsh contrast. *Sickness Unto Death* performs a similar function. Despair may be neither as needed nor as extreme as S.K. paints it in his psychological analysis, but the task of becoming a self and making decisions against the infinity of possibility can only be faced if harsh measures are introduced. Just as the self requires constant and ceaseless effort if it is not to be lost, so there is never a time when the lack of a corrective is not a danger.

In the *Philosophical Fragments* S.K. portrays Socrates and his questions as the corrective needed against those who think they can find truth too easily. But we also discover the necessity of seeing truth in even more radical terms. This situation is the religious context of man's need for salvation or restoration. God becomes our corrective because he alone can serve as our teacher, since only he who has the power to alter the very being of the learner radically can teach him.

In a fitting piece of irony, S.K. becomes his own corrective in *The Point of View.* In that work he tries to alter our perspective on the whole of his writing, and he argues that his collected works are not to be viewed as one might naturally have supposed. S.K. corrects himself, but in the process he forces the reader to supply his own corrective. Now the reader must evaluate S.K.'s works as a whole and determine both the relation of the author to the work and the relation of the reader to the author.

If S.K. had allowed his works to stand without adding his own commentary, they might simply have been absorbed as written. His own outcry in the *Attack,* and his revision of his own purposes in *Point of View,* force the reader into a reappraisal he might not otherwise have stirred himself to make. S.K. corrects himself as he corrects others, but we know that his own supplied corrective need not be—in fact cannot be—literal truth. The aim of corrective is to force us to rethink any too easy assumption, and the only way to do that is to take an extreme position. S.K. does this, and it opens him to criticism. But it also opens the reader to correction—both from himself and from the author.

Of course, with Kierkegaard the whole question of "authorship" and "corrective" are bound up with his complex notion of "direct communication." We discover this most prominently in his use of pseudonyms for himself in his early publications. S.K. tells us that authorship must be indirect, to make the reader take responsibility and to face himself, not the author, directly. But this is not a simple matter, as little about S.K.'s authorship is, because later he switches to direct communication and admits his authorship of the earlier pseudonymous works. S.K. gives his reasons for doing this, but the question at the moment is to understand the function of an author and how corrective is best applied. We know that a direct attack on the reader is not recommended at first, because it simply sets up a reaction and the author will be dismissed. Thus, any successful authorship cannot be completely straightforward.

S.K. realizes that Christianity involves witnessing which brings him to speak out directly, but his whole work shows the tension between witnessing and the indirect communication his existential position requires, if responsibility is to be placed on the reader to decide. Direct communication is not superior to indirect, although it certainly would make life (and interpreting Kierkegaard) easier if it were. S.K. confesses that he simply did not know his plan in advance and so could not state the plan of his authorship directly. It became clear only later, although he nevertheless subjects his reader to the confusion of accounting for his authorship at the end as if he knew its purpose from the beginning. Thus, direct communication is clarifying in one sense but confusing in another, if it pretends that what was not known directly at an earlier time was.

Kierkegaard's position on whether or not he himself is a "Christian" is a good case in point. We know that he thinks the outward observance of Christianity is unimportant and at worst deceptive. So that to assert one's "Christianity" is to miss the point that verbal confession and outward form are not the issue. But if Christianity has become confused with ritual and outward appearance, then he thinks real Christianity must be reintroduced by one who says that he himself is not a Christian. If this is true, when S.K. denies or questions whether he is a Christian, ought we simply to accept this? Or, is it the "deceit" and the "indirectness" required of an author if he is to communicate? That is, S.K.'s own "Christianity" is not the issue, or else it could be stated with proper qualifications. But if it is the reader's "Christianity" that is the issue, and if it is not easy to make him face it, the author sacrifices directness for an indirect means in order to raise the issue and communicate his point.

The question is whether "corrective" is best accomplished by straightforward statement. It is clear that S.K. thinks direct communication—at least at first—risks rejection and will fail its task. The author must first establish a relationship, even at the risk of some confusion over his person or his intent. The author sacrifices the reader's understanding of the author, hopefully to increase the reader's better understanding of himself. The author who is only anxious to make his own position clear ("Let me make one thing perfectly clear") may end in confusing his reader about where the issue lies. Since such an author may intend deception by the use of clarity, indirect communication is more intricate, but in the long run it is a more truthful and instructive form of authorship.

Christ / Christianity

Understanding certainty and change have been prime metaphysical questions since at least the time Parmenides and Plato debated the problems involved. One does not tend to think of these puzzling concepts as of such central concern to Kierkegaard, due to his anti-metaphysical stance in opposition to Hegel. However, it is an illuminating sidelight to see how S.K. treats certainty and change, since both figure as strong undercurrents in his writing. We know that in man's relationship to God, he vehemently denies that certainty is possible. This is the basis of his whole existential analysis of the uncertainty inherent in the human situation. This poses the difficult problem of achieving faith, since certainty is unavailable and makes faith a heroic task. It must be admired and held on to in the face of constant uncertainty.

This situation worries Kierkegaard in relation to the task of the apostle, whom he takes to be one called by a revelation of which he has an immediate certainty. When we look carefully, it is not so easy as to say that all of life is uncertain, because on the other hand S.K. is conscious of the finality of the Christian claim. Thus, it is more accurate to say that man lives in never-ending tension between the uncertainty of his own situation and the awareness of the certainty of God's demands and his own action. You cannot reach an immediate certainty about whether you (or S.K.) have faith, for faith is a dialectical suspension which constantly involves fear and trembling. In fact, faith means to continue and not to fall into despair in such a situation, in spite of the impossibility of certainty and yet its unrelenting demand nevertheless.

Thus, we have another explanation of why Kierkegaard is so ambivalent about calling himself a Christian. It is not a state about which you can pronounce with certainty, and it may change from moment to moment. In fact, "to be a Christian" is to maintain faith in spite of the impossibility of being certain, which at least means that one cannot be certain about being a Christian. However, the tension of man's uncertainty is brought about partly by S.K.'s traditional view of God's own certainty. S.K. radicalizes human existence, but he leaves God's certainty beyond question. In fact, we miss the religious side of S.K.'s nature if we do not realize the enormous underlying sense of confidence S.K. has in God's certainty, as he expresses this in his religious discourses. It is only philosophically and psychologically that man experiences uneradicable uncertainty. This does not occur religiously where God's nature is seen, although the contrast between the two is a painful situation.

"Change," S.K. tells us, is the transition from possibility to actuality. As such it is outside God's experience but is at the very heart of human existence. "The past," of course, is the realm of certainty, but it also brings on illusion if the pattern discerned in the past in retrospect is applied to the present. What has happened has happened and cannot be undone, but strictly speaking this is not a change into necessity, since it came from an original uncertainty. What was uncertain cannot change into the necessary, for what is necessary cannot change and come into existence where once it was not. Thus, if men act in order to make their potential existence concrete, they do not remain unchanged, and human existence cannot be called necessary. Human nature is changed essentially as it comes into existence.

Possibility is a state of non-being that is changed by coming into existence, so that its actualization can never be called necessary. Coming into existence involves a change in actuality, so that whatever comes into existence shows by that fact that it is not necessary. Necessity therefore cannot be used to qualify existence. God's own life, of course, is lived in contrast to this. Since he is not involved in this flux, one cannot come closer to God by changing one's place. Thus, man becomes aware of his problem of relating to God. Man lives in uncertainty and possibility and change while God does not. How can such uncertainty find a relationship to that whose existence is based on a contrasting order? Some have tried to embrace human existence under a scheme of necessity, as a way of bringing God's and man's life together, but S.K. rejects this easy way of reconciling the tension.

Change is our lot, but it is also the origin of our freedom. Since necessity is excluded from our life, we are free to use possibilities to create life as we will—if we take decisive action in time. We have no necessary essence we must fulfill, but this flexibility places us in extreme tension in relation to God. Where change and certainty are concerned, S.K. rejects any proposal that reduces one to the other level. They remain in tension and in paradox, and that is the plane on which human existence is acted out. To escape by denying either is to try to shift the burden of responsibility that belongs to man. Religiously, it is the burden God has given man. Uncertainty touches all that has life and change excludes necessity. Yet to relate to necessity and that which does not change is the Promethean task assigned to all who will accept their humanity and not run from it.

Happy/Unhappy

His readers grow used to Kierkegaard speaking about Christianity and Christendom, but not so used to thinking of him speaking about Christ or the person of Jesus. Given the Old Testament theme he employs in *Fear and Trembling,* his famous definition of the life of the Knight of Faith does not involve Jesus in any direct way. Christ as the mediator between God and man does not seem to be a strong theme in S.K.'s dealings with God. Instead, man seems to stand alone directly before God without benefit of mediation. On the other hand, an examination of S.K.'s references to Christ in his writings reveals that it is a common theme. After making Christianity into an almost impossible achievement, he will say quite easily in another moment that Christ's life is simply the norm for the Christian to follow.

True, in good existential fashion Kierkegaard makes Jesus' activity, not his words, the principal thing that defines his life. Those who are truly regenerate will find that similar activity unfolds in them. S.K. has had trouble with the doctrine of God's incarnation, and he represents the paradox of the eternal becoming temporal as the chief stumbling block to faith in *Fear and Trembling.* But in speaking of Jesus' life, he simply reports that Christ's birth is the greatest anthropomorphism, and this does not seem to trouble him. Jesus clearly is easier for S.K. to relate to than God, but he does not seem to follow tradition in finding the former a way to God. He makes Jesus quite human in refusing to see his death as fixed by God in advance. Jesus simply was willing to offer his life. It is out of love for men, S.K. thinks, that Jesus did not prevent men from murdering him. Biblical scholarship is not the way; one only learns who Jesus is by prayerfully turning himself to Jesus.

The real issue, S.K. says, is to present Jesus as he walked and lived 1,800 years ago, which does not sound as difficult as the problem of the "contemporary disciple" which he agonized over in his *Philosophical Fragments*. He does mention Jesus as the sign of offense, but the offense is not so much in the intellectual problem of the eternal becoming temporal as it is in the cultural offense of putting God together with a socially insignificant man. Yet S.K. seems able to resolve this more easily in speaking about Christ than in understanding Abraham. He simply says that the eternal in Jesus is the compounding of insignificance with being God. Yet he merges this with the later theme of *Attack* by saying no secular advantage must be gained by preaching about Christ, since his insignificance is central to being Christian. True, Jesus kept the people in unremitting tension, so that S.K.'s interpretation of the life of Jesus has an existential flavor.

There is a collision between divine and human qualities, but the emphasis is not so much on the intellectual difficulties involved as it is on Christ coming to save us and to present an example. He is the prototype himself, which makes it sound as if approaching Christ is far easier than approaching God. S.K. stresses that the belief in the Second Coming helps one endure the agony involved in being a Christian, but this is an aid he did not mention in defining Christianity more abstractly in the *Postscript*. Although what is essentially Christian is still analogous to madness, it is Jesus' enduring suffering and not protesting it that marks him out as the son of God, S.K. is convinced. Jesus' decision not to help himself and summon legions of angels proves his divinity as he-who-accepts-suffering silently.

Christ did not establish theological doctrine; he acted. Thus, dogmatics should not be an intellectual creation but must grow out of Christ's activity. Yet the irony is that the Christian is taken to be a man with a particular fixed idea. Christianity is essentially the mediated relationship through which man must always approach the divine. To be sure, brilliant minds and deep thinkers have been Christians, but this is distorted when boundaries are set up by a pope or when Christians attempt to hit others over the head with the Bible or a creed. Christianity should come to us in humble insignificance in order not to distress us with its magnificence. True, Christianity still requires subjectivity and exists in the individual's subjective acceptance, but this account makes it not quite so difficult to achieve as it is if we take the *Postscript* alone.

In Kierkegaardian fashion, Jesus is portrayed as one who in his life bore the heavy cross of misunderstanding. This continues S.K.'s existential emphasis on the necessity for and the edifying consequences of being misunderstood. This misunderstanding is necessary since truth cannot be conveyed directly. S.K. has stressed the rarity of the true Christian. However, it is not well recognized that he does not accept this as desirable but rather insists that a desperate missionary effort is all the more needed to make men aware. He continues his notion that the true Christian is always a martyr, but the extremity of the view of *Attack*— that one must be killed—is not always stressed. It is as difficult to become a Christian in 1848 as in the year 1. But the other side of this statement, which is often missed, is that it continues to be possible for thousands to become Christian.

Christianity is not a doctrine, not something to be lectured about, to quarrel over as men quarrel over what Platonic philosophy is. It is an existential-communication, something to be lived out and acted. Christianity can only be presented by existing—a definition which takes it out of the realm of an intellectual puzzle, although that is the impression S.K. sometimes conveys. When S.K. says he has never seen a Christian, he does not mean its intellectual impossibility. He means that the Christian life must express that there is an absolute, and he has not seen one whose life fully expressed this. Sometimes S.K. is thought to make Christianity into an affair that requires the strength of genius, but he specifically says it relates itself to the common man.

Since Christianity requires that its follower love men with his whole heart, it is bound to be rewarded with persecution. In the *Attack*, Kierkegaard relates Christianity to being a witness to the truth in a way that could cause some to overlook its essential requirement of love. Still, becoming a Christian involves the laughable paradox that the absolute has come to exist in this world, so that suffering is involved in becoming a Christian. Human reason is lost and crucified on this paradox. However, one becomes a Christian not because he is challenged to achieve an intellectual feat but because he has become conscious of sin. To want to become a Christian for any other reason than a sense of sin is literally foolishness, not the violation of some law of logic. For this reason Christianity means an end to happy and pleasant days. To love God in earnest involves being badly treated by men.

As S.K. has said repeatedly, Christianity is not more true now because there are so many million Christians. The difficulty of the individual in taking the step is the same then and today. If it seems otherwise, it is a false Christianity and the impetus is not the anguish of a sense of sin. The life is so difficult to live that miracles are needed now more than ever. Christianity as a doctrine is not impossible to understand. What is difficult is the degree of self-overcoming and renunciation which it demands. When the anxiety of sin and the burdened conscience constrain a man to cross the narrow line between despair and madness—this is Christianity, not some intellectual puzzle or proof of God's existence.

S.K. sometimes talks of martyrdom as a necessity, but it is the absolute offer of the self he means to stress, not the strict loss of life. You are anxious before Christ even though you offer yourself to him. Christendom is not Christianity; that distinction is always clear. The art, the glory of Christendom is quite other than sin and the personal suffering of the individual Christian. Tranquility is thus not the medium to communicate Christianity because it is coextensive with personal anxiety. To be eloquent in presenting Christianity is fine, but, to express it existentially, it is as if you had blown up the world and people are scandalized. People are deeply moved if you preach, but if you give your possessions to the poor they are scandalized. Christianity has been too much changed into a consolation. We have forgotten it is a requirement.

In regard to existential knowing, the main thing is to bring about the situation, and so it is with Christianity. Christianity is attractive enough at first glance, but you need Christ's help when you try to live it. Christianity involves so much self-denial that it cannot be particularly inviting to the world in general. Christianity is not a doctrine. It is an existence communication. The choice you have is whether to act it out or not, and reflection cannot get hold of that solution. Christianity, being God's invention, cannot be taken over by men. God decided to become man in order to have compassion for men. The human race has advanced, but there are no more today who are able to be bearers of Christianity than before. Since God is a spirit, only one who has died to the physical world can learn to speak that language.

We try to get God's love for ourselves in order to lead a cozy existence. In reality, to resolve to love God is *ipso facto* to die to the world. Thus, most people leave the matter of Christianity undecided, because its requirements are puzzling to them. Later Christians, who now have the invented help of sacraments, excuse themselves from loving God. The Christian sacraments survive, the customs and the terminology, but these are decorations. They are presented to us by the preacher-actor-artist playing at Christianity, and such showmanship should be included in the list of heresies. Instead of letting life go the way it was going, what the God of Christianity wanted was a world-transformation. This is why those who continue to hold on to the ways of the world have such a hard time understanding the mission of Christ and what is involved in becoming a Christian.

Certainty/Change

"Existence" and "existential" are the two terms we most commonly associate with Kierkegaard, but he does not use them often. The terms a man becomes famous for are not always the ones he himself uses most frequently. Yet S.K. does speak of existence in a unique way at times. Of course he does not call himself an "existentialist," but the name is not misapplied if we refer to Kierkegaard. The endless questions about "what I am," this is the existential condition for S.K. But the main point is his conviction that life can be interpreted only after it has been experienced, not before. The scientific and historical modes of analysis developed by the modern world hoped to overcome this limitation on human understanding by using historical material or scientific data. "Existentialism" chiefly means the denial of our ability to understand life in advance of its being lived out, no matter what sophisticated tools we employ.

There is no way to achieve understanding except to go through the experience oneself. The poet can express in words what he has experienced beautifully. That is his art. But however much we may drink in the words and appreciate them aesthetically, our depth of understanding is not increased until we pass through the same experience ourselves. The religious poet is nearly driven mad by God, and to understand this the reader must go through the same experience of being burned by nearness to God. The poet's fate is to know a thirst which is never satisfied, so it would be an ironical reversal if, by simply listening to descriptions of the religious life, one found himself satiated. The result of hearing the biblical-poetic-religious word should be to instill in the hearer a restlessness, a thirst, a search. And the same thing essentially holds true of most aspects of life.

Philosophy should tell us that life must be understood backwards, but it should also go on to warn us that it must be lived forward. Only decisive human action yields a pattern which can be analyzed. Following the way of life of another, or listless drifting, does not do it. Existence is always a tragedy in the beginning, but it can turn into a vaudeville act. That is, one must come to life and act it out as a comedy with entertainment. In relation to existence there is only one schoolmaster, existence itself. We cannot be taught about this before we live it through, or at least what we have been told only acquires meaning as we live it through. We can learn all kinds of things about various problems in advance. But if it is an existential problem, the main issue is its significance to me, and that cannot be told to me by anyone else.

The problem is that what we think about increases in difficulty in proportion to the existential use a person puts it to. Thus, what is of no personal significance is the easiest to comprehend, but that of the greatest personal importance offers the most difficulty. As S.K. often charges, Hegel as a man exists in categories entirely different from those in which he speculates as a philosopher. Thus, he can seem to solve complex problems easily, but they are in fact unrelated to the immediacies of his existence. S.K. complains about philosophers who think in entirely different categories from those in which they live. Thought can divorce itself from the immediacies of life, but then it is not existential.

S.K.'s goal was to leave behind very accurate and experiencially based observations concerning the conditions of existence, versus other philosophers whom he thinks avoid this or divorce themselves from it by abstract thought. His discovery was the denial of the doctrine of progress and evolution, so dear to the hearts of many 19th century thinkers. S.K. was convinced that the conditions of existence are everywhere the same for all men. Time and place in historical sequence do not change this. Sartre will transform his point to say that there is no universal human essence but only a common human condition. Thus, all men are the same in existential situation, and their historical time and place does not aid their existential understanding, however important accumulated wisdom and science may be otherwise.

The only foolish one is one who does not venture far enough to learn from existence. Guilt comes only from not having ventured far enough out, not so much from specific acts. One can be wise in books, brilliant in speculation, and foolish in never having ventured in life. Genuine decisions never happen to a man. You have to enter into the decision itself—that is the source of the existential notion that there can be no such thing as objective determination where existential problems are concerned. To say this does not deny that there are many objective issues which are perfectly capable of being determined on that basis, but it does say that the problems of human existence cannot be determined without subjective involvement. Existence is such that it demands involvement for understanding where mathematics or geography or cooking do not.

It is the "spectator theory of knowledge" which Kierkegaard cannot abide. As American pragmatists argue, you must participate in knowledge, apply it and try it for yourself, if you would learn. The passive observer may pick up much information but no existential understanding. In fact, the desire to remain a neutral observer in life is for S.K. the chief sin. One is looking for enjoyment when earnestness is required. Existence is so ordered that it requires examination, self-denial, a test of power. Force is required, and it must be applied individually. You can study history, but in the deepest sense no one can really learn from history. You only learn by applying power yourself. When you venture far out, then you stand in the situation of actuality.

Human imagination is too weak for existence. It cannot reproduce the actual pressures of finite existence. They must be lived through. Ideas cannot mirror existence, even if they contain much of its content and something of value. Living in ideas is the very contradiction to living in actuality, but to live in books is the philosopher's constant temptation. The only essential sermon one can listen to and appropriate comes not from the pulpit via the minister's words but from one's own existence. This is the message of existentialism. Existence corresponds to the individual, not the concept of the universal. To conceptualize is to dissolve existence into possibility and away from actuality. As far as contact with actuality is concerned, to increase our powers of conceptualization is a step backwards.

The aim is to move from possibility toward actuality, that is, to determine a concrete action. To do that is to face existence, but conceptualization diverts our attention into thought and to considering still more new possibilities. This subverts the needed decision, unless we are careful to guard against the dangers of a purely intellectual existence. For instance, to transform Christianity into "science and scholarship" is an error, since if it succeeds Christianity will be abolished. Its existence lies on another plane of individual decisiveness. Christianity is not a doctrine but an "existence communication." It must be perceived in that way as a problem, not as a scientific study or a matter for scholars to debate.

Artists-in-eloquence may cover over what it means to exist, but the more a person himself strives in daily existence, the less he will be inclined to deliver speeches. He will realize their inappropriateness where action is the issue. The very meaning of existence is to be under constant examination. God is actually amused by the leaping and surging and twisting of the millions of people who try to get hold of truth without having to suffer. This S.K. defines as the core of existentialism: Existence is ordered in such a way that truly to relate oneself to truth is impossible without suffering, if the truth is related to the individual. Where Christianity is concerned, S.K. thinks it has gained the ease and comfortableness and indolence reserved for triviality. And Christianity above all is an existential matter for S.K. and thus cannot be understood in this way, much less lived out.

One way to understand how Kierkegaard conceives of existence is to see the importance he gives to "the moment." It is, of course, his way of opposing Hegel's confidence in historical and systematic understanding as the way to solve the puzzle of existence. That is, Hegel wants to set the contemporary issue in a time framework, and he counts on the insights history reveals to guide our present decisions. In contrast, S.K. wants to stress the significance of the moment and its decisiveness. When matters of your own life and its future shape are concerned, there comes a time (a moment) when you stand alone. Then it is yours to decide without external aid. Of course, you can reject this burden thrust upon you and either let external events determine the decision or pretend some historical destiny controls it, but then the individual loses all decisiveness and character in that moment.

When the moment comes to have such decisive significance, the person is essentially alone and the outcome cannot be attributed to outside forces. Of course, obscure forces within the individual can be allowed to determine the moment, but then the decision is not authentic and the individual's character is not formed in the action; he or she drifts. S.K. associates "the leap" with the decisive moment. That is, the transition is not smooth and follows no inevitable logic. Rather, the individual resolve alone carries the individual across the moment to a decisive conclusion. Existence (vs. history and science and scholarship) has no smooth flow. It is the achievement (or the failure) based on human decisiveness brought to bear in the few crucial moments thrust upon us.

Existence/The Moment

Happy and unhappy are terms we think of first in connection with S.K.'s *Journals* (trans. Alexander Dru, New York: Harper & Bros., 1959). It is here that he speaks most candidly of his unhappiness and his attempt to find happiness in spite of his melancholy and remorse. However, these concepts figure heavily in the less autobiographical writings of S.K. too, just as most important aspects of his personality do.

Happiness and unhappiness are also tied to inwardness, that most crucial of all the religious concepts which S.K. stressed. Externally considered, his life seems by all accounts to have been a happy one, so that it is to his inwardness that we must turn if we want to understand what unhappiness is and what produces it. Thus, happiness-unhappiness are connected with, although perhaps not parallel to, the problem of inner-outer.

The aesthetic, the ethical, and the religious phases of life are also intimately connected with happiness and unhappiness. Thus, this pair of opposites cuts across the heart of S.K.'s writing, just as it cuts across his life. "Inwardly torn asunder as I was," S.K. tells us in that now classic passage, "without any expectation of leading a happy earthly life . . ." (*Journals,* IV, 1836–37, p. 40 Dru). And he goes on to say that this situation forced him to cling only to the intellectual side in man. Yet he lived very comfortably in bourgeois Copenhagen and did not even have to earn his living because of an inheritance from his father. We know, therefore, that the source of his unhappiness was not so much external as internal, which is what in fact he tells us. If a man is ever capable of living totally outside of himself, happiness might be his.

S.K. tells us that he wants to find the truth which is true for him, for which he can live and die (Aug. 1, 1835). We can also see that he is happy (and others are too) just to the extent that he can realize this goal—and he is unhappy just to the extent that he cannot. However, we know that such effort is never complete, for in a sense S.K. finally did find the idea, or ideas, which were true for him. This single idea was to reintroduce Christianity into Christendom, or to complete the inward reformation left unfinished by Martin Luther. In spite of this, at the time he dies S.K. is at the peak of his unhappiness. Thus, to find such a true idea is important to happiness, but its achievement is neither finished nor does it guarantee happiness. And more important, its actual implementation is a more difficult project than simply imbedding it in thought.

S.K. comments on the importance of wit and humor, and his writings abound in examples. Yet he still connects wit with despair, announcing that, after a successful party at which he furnished the entertainment, he wanted to shoot himself (1836, Dru p. 51). Since one cannot cheat and copy the answers to life's problems from someone else, happiness is more difficult to achieve if we are forced to experiment and do life by trial and error. A safe inherited formula would make happiness easier, but S.K. is convinced that even such a life cannot be secure against despair. We can grieve over life's inequities, if we have the moral courage to do so, but only with religious courage can we rejoice. All of this tells us that the religious dimension brings its own problems. However, it also carries a certain form of happiness, even if this is not a life of pure pleasure.

Of course, it is S.K.'s broken engagement with Regine, plus his never realized desire to be a country parson, which provides his own greatest stumbling block to achieving happiness. He broke the engagement: she did not. Thus, it was within his own power to marry, just as no one held him back from becoming a country parson. This tells us—which S.K. would be the first to point out—that unhappiness springs from an inner disproportion in the man, not from external circumstances or restraints. His own inner despair kept him from involving others in it. His own intense and profitable struggle with religion made it impossible for him to express it in any simple external life, although to do this could bring him happiness. What he wished to be lay outside of himself and at a distance from what he was, and such a state produces unhappiness.

Regine, of course, tells S.K. that he can never be happy. The issue, therefore, is not so much to search for a happiness which cannot be as it is to try to find a way to make unhappiness religiously and artistically fruitful. Desire fulfilled is not necessarily happiness, since S.K.'s "desire" was to be married and to be a country parson, and yet he did neither. To become a self, as we know all too well, is a difficult task.

Evidently it is the complexity of the self's structure which prevents us from satisfying any desire simply and thereby finding happiness. No one thing can of itself bring happiness, because the self is not a unity given to us at the outset of life. Yet we seek individual satisfactions in spite of this. Unfortunately, we never know in advance how our attempts will turn out. We can only understand after the effort is over, and still we think that, if only we could understand at the outset, this would produce happiness.

To have a systematic philosophy and a profound understanding of life might seem to make us happy. Yet as men our lives must still be lived outside such neat orders and intelligence. "In relation to their systems most systematizers are like a man who builds an enormous castle and lives in a shack close by" (1846). This is the "existential distance," the estrangement between life and thought. It is also the essential alienation which marks S.K.'s career, and it is the source of all his basic unhappiness over life.

S.K. is convinced that not a single person understands him. However, due to the isolation of the individual and the essential alienation of life from thought, this really cannot be otherwise. Only he who is fully understood by another can be happy, and only he who can completely lose himself in the enjoyment of the moment without reflection can be happy. Neither are possible for S.K., nor is it possible for most men to find such unity—except perhaps in a fleeting moment. But even when it comes, this is not enough to satisfy life's hunger.

One understands and is understood better after the experience is over, but happiness demands either advance or present understanding. In his March, 1846 report S.K. gives the classic definition of his unhappiness: "I am in the profoundest sense an unhappy individuality which from its earliest years has been nailed fast to some suffering or other, bordering upon madness, and which must have its deeper roots in a disproportion between soul and body." Unhappiness is connected to the source of suffering, and this comes about because the mind and body are not parallel attributes, as Spinoza thought they were. They are actually different kinds of substances which do not behave according to the same laws. Thus, soul and body are seldom happy together nor do they share the same kinds of happiness.

Nevertheless, the drive to authorship stems from the despair over achieving happiness, so that unhappiness is not without its significant and fruitful side. S.K. listed his ideals as "to marry and to become a country parson," but it is his despair over achieving these which drove him to become an author. The happiness-unhappiness dichotomy, then, is itself the source of insight and not at all to be despised, however constantly uncomfortable it may be to live through. Yet his melancholy still drives him to want to be nothing. It is not so much the source of authorship as it is of the constant tension and struggle to be happy and to overcome unhappiness. The understanding can never complete its task, except to understand that there are things it cannot understand. This is a road to which there is no end, just as authorship has no conclusion except the arbitrary one of death.

"The individual" is the category S.K. wants to name as his own (May, 1847), but no one may be happy alone. To be a poet means to have one's personal life in quite different categories from one's poetic work. Ironically, that which is the source of poetic inspiration is also the source of the poet's unhappiness over not being able to be at one with himself. S.K. adopts a poetic means of communication, but it stems from the fact that he can never be at one with his work. Nor can he as a person ever be happy by simply being the author of his books. It may be necessary for him to communicate poetically and it may be the only true means, but it does place the writer at a distance from both his work and his readers. This quite possibly is the source of S.K.'s greatest unhappiness over being an author.

Christianity, as S.K. interprets it, is the source of some happiness but also of much unhappiness. The Knight of Faith in *Fear and*

Trembling can neither make himself known to, nor can he communicate with, anyone else. "Believing by virtue of the absurd" is not only a difficult thing to do, but it deprives the one who performs that act of total happiness. The inward spiritual renewal, of which S.K. thought himself to be the prophet, is a more difficult and also a less obvious task.

Since Christianity demands suffering and some form of martyrdom, it does not bring with it the easy state which happiness requires. It is true that in his edifying discourses S.K. achieves a serenity and a repose like that of most devotional and spiritual writers. Thus, one might say that the struggle to achieve faith is fierce and has its unhappy aspects, but the religious life, once achieved, can be full of satisfying and even happy moments. Of course, just as the essay on "Equilibrium" in *Either/Or* describes the difficult balance between the aesthetical and the ethical in the composition of personality, so the addition of the religious dimension involves a more arduous task to maintain equilibrium. Since no Hegelian higher synthesis of opposites is possible, we know that no permanent happy solution is attainable. Yet it is also true that moments of happiness can be achieved just insofar as it is possible to accomplish a momentary equilibrium between the various sides of man. Of course, the ethical demand, the aesthetic demand and the religious demand each differ and are somewhat at odds. Every moment of happiness rests on a precarious balance that always tends to slip away.

The aesthetic life (Vol. I, *Either/Or*) is, of course, S.K.'s proposal for a way to achieve happiness, and he describes this skill in his essay on "The Rotation Method." He who can achieve and master the art of aesthetic existence can be happy on that plane, because the aesthetic life depends on the enjoyment of immediacy. However, one of the problems involved in achieving happiness, and also the cause of unhappiness, is the difficult technique necessary to maintain such a life, plus the tendency of ethical and religious concerns to break in with demands that destroy the aesthetic mood, e.g., marriage, despair. Thus, what constitutes happiness on one plane may not produce it on the other. Happiness itself is difficult because it is not one thing, and only he who can "will one thing" can ever be truly at peace with himself.

However, the short piece on "The Unhappiest Man" in the first volume of *Either/Or* is perhaps S.K.'s classic text on the nature of happiness-unhappiness and the sources of these moods. This short piece also gives us a good indication of S.K.'s relationship to Hegel, since he borrows his theme from and compares it with Hegel's essay on the "unhappiest consciousness." Briefly, what S.K. wants to show is that Job in his grief is not the epitome of the unhappy consciousness. God has spoken to him, and thus Job has a religious significance in his past which cannot be taken away no matter what happens to him. Nor is anyone completely unhappy, no matter what his present condition, if it is possible to look forward to any future happiness. A significant past or an open future each give life a certain meaning, and thus they defeat the ultimate condition of unhappiness—a total absence of all meaning.

S.K. makes the comment that one is edified by considering the wretchedness of life (Vol. I, p. 180). He gives voice to the existential theme that, where understanding is the goal, happiness is less instructive to insight than unhappiness. "The unhappy person is the one who has his ideal, the content of his life, the fullness of his consciousness, the essence of his being, in some manner outside of himself" (*ibid.,* p. 181). He is always absent and never present to himself.

Thus, S.K. has revealed the depths of the origin of unhappiness. And we also discover the unobtainableness of happiness for anything beyond the moment. Its ineradicable source lies in the basic disproportion of Being itself. In the self, unhappiness stems from the lack of correspondence between ideal notions and real existence. Furthermore, meaninglessness and lack of hope are the other conditions which produce unhappiness, so that unhappiness is related to both non-being and the source of our failure to achieve meaning. Yet one cannot wish for life to be totally full of meaning and hope and past significance. Even that is not one's ideal. Existence is still estranged from what potentially could give meaning. Furthermore, what is instructive does not alone make us happy. For one who seeks to understand his existence, the alteration of mood knows no end.

S.K. has thus given us a psychological content to Hegel's abstract definition of unhappiness. Simply to know an intellectual formula is not enough. One must experience unhappiness for himself and know it in the depth of an interior mood. Existence involves more than thought. In fact, basic unhappiness stems from the fact that what one knows as true in thought is never quite the same in experience, and this unbridgeable gap keeps happiness at a distance.

In his writings which came to form *Attack Upon Christendom* (trans. Walter Lowrie, Princeton University Press, 1946), we discover another source of S.K.'s unhappiness. In his later years, he became restless and unable to restrain himself from "speaking out." Thus, if one becomes a "witness to the truth," he foregoes a great deal of happiness because he feels forced to cause a disturbance in the interests of seeing truth spoken. To attack the establishment, or to disturb the serenity of society and its ways, is to ask for trouble. Furthermore, S.K. finally defines a witness to the truth as a "martyr." If this is true, one cannot pursue both happiness and the truth. Suffering is involved in a truth which demands that the comforts of society be opposed.

However, in *Sickness Unto Death* (trans. Walter Lowrie, New York: Doubleday Anchor, 1954) we encounter S.K.'s views on the problems of the self and discover the basic origins of happiness and unhappiness. In the first place, those who pursue Christianity must realize they have less happiness in front of them. This is not simply because they come near adopting the martyr's life, but it is because they also must announce the essential sickness of the self to others. Dread and despair and courage are more the marks of Christian existence than happiness.

The spirit of man must synthesize the finite and the infinite. But this is essentially an impossible task, since happiness still depends on complete oneness with oneself. God is involved in relating the self to a power beyond itself, so that, if God must be involved, happiness and unhappiness become far from a simple affair. To be sick but to be able to cultivate these disproportions between finite and infinite, possibility and necessity, is an advantage to man. It is a divine gift to possess a spirit, but it makes happiness a difficult state and despair almost a natural one. Moreover, necessity constantly enters in by pressing the self to become a self it does not want to be. This pushes the self toward despair and away from the ideal self it desires to be, which would be its happiness.

To the extent that any ideal lies outside actual existence, all men are in despair whether they recognize it or not. One can be unaware of this. You can think yourself happy and discover that the mood did not go deep enough to sustain itself as you had hoped. There can be imaginary happiness. The great difficulty, however, is that clinging to immediate happiness hides despair and its source in the basic disproportion of soul. Thus, one who seeks momentary satisfaction may actually feel happiness. Yet he must face the task of fusing possibility and necessity, and this only creates a deeper despair that eventually breaks through the cover of immediate happiness.

The task of forming the self can be avoided by the aesthetic life, if one can conceal the hidden forms of despair that develop from not creating the self one has the opportunity to forge and become. We will not venture for fear of loss, and yet we may lose the self by failing to test it in a venture. The real source of happiness or unhappiness lies in the task of constantly becoming a true self.

Individual/The Mass

S.K. has made famous his category of "the individual," which he wants to press against Hegel's emphasis on "the mass" in world events. S.K. told his readers he wanted only one inscription on his tombstone, "The Individual" (which is not the way it actually reads). In religion, he stressed the aloneness of the individual before God, until it almost became an obsession with him to detach religion from all community or group practice. Since Kierkegaard's time, the term "alienation" has come into prominence, and a great deal of this stems from his psychological analysis of the isolation of the individual and the individual's essential aloneness in his interior and subjective life. S.K. stressed the radical separation of inner from outer. This means that, if the individual is essentially identified with the inner life, he finds himself alienated from others whose outer shell alone is visible.

There is really only one single quality, S.K. tells us, "individuality." And truth means that everyone must make a personal accounting to God. Quiet and protracted intimacy with oneself brings isolation, partly because religiousness means to speak quite softly with oneself. The corrupt form of escape from all this is to want to hide in the mass or the crowd. God, S.K. is convinced, does not talk to men in an assembly but only to each one individually. Christianity, of course, is accessible to all. It is just that it occurs through and only through each one becoming an individual. "The single individual" the category through which, in a religious sense, the age and the generation must move. "The single individual"—with this category the cause of Christianity stands or falls, S.K. tells his readers.

But you cannot teach anyone about this category directly, S.K. adds. Thus, he brings us back to his stress on the need for indirect modes of communication. We can see that indirect expression is necessary, because it protects the privacy and integrity of the individual. Only the individual can relate himself truly to God, so religiously a loss of individuality involves the loss of God. Men escape God by sociality, as everyone who is driven away from religion to social work should confess. In a time of agitation, inwardness must be strengthened by leading each individual to an indifference to external change. The category of the single individual always relates to inward deepening, just as social involvement leads to spiritual superficiality. God can only move a generation through individuality. Take it away and God is dethroned.

God too dwells in solitude, S.K. is convinced. Men must learn to tolerate this if they want to amount to anything. Only the single individual can be in kinship with God, never the group. When life is jointly shared, there is an alleviation of suffering and freedom from concern, it is true, but this also leads away from God. As S.K. often said of his writings, each book sought only one reader, a single individual, one who would read it as a personal communication from the author. Of course, everyone can become a single individual. It is just that it must be done alone and not in groups. One must withdraw as a single individual, alone before God—this is S.K.'s frequent theme at its most extreme. For traditionalists, it is interesting that S.K. does not mention Jesus or any mediator, but leaves man entirely alone before God.

Christianity teaches the fall of the race and the resurrection of the individual, S.K. remarks in a graphic phrase which illustrates his point. Joining a group is a way of getting rid of conscience, but a strong conscience is a necessary prerequisite to conversion, so joining the crowd weakens our chance to induce repentance. Everyone wants to obligate others to the theology he creates, but this makes for confusion, since the point is to be obligated to the New Testament. The point is not to obligate others but to feel your own obligation and, most important, to express it in action. The source of heresy in Christianity really lies in "the church," since all discussion of groups lessens the real thrust of Christianity toward action and diverts attention to doctrine and organization. The issue is not to introduce a new doctrine into the world but to appropriate a given doctrine personally in inward deepening.

The single individual must understand himself and his action in relation to God, which makes him extraordinary if he does. But it is hard to persevere standing alone, and even Luther gave in and could not forbear founding a party. Then, in a short time Lutheranism became another externality and as much a matter of rote as Catholicism ever was. Christianity's core is not to be found in rituals but in divine love that makes every human being into an individual. God could act as a sovereign before us and issue divine commands. Instead he humbles human sovereignty and uses only single individuals as instruments. S.K. is so strongly anti-group that he asserts Christianity does not join men together in groups but separates them, in order to unite every single individual with God.

In place of mass conversion, S.K. tells us that Christianity begins when one is saved, one among millions, one in the whole world. But we must stop and ask Kierkegaard if this fascinating doctrine of his is really what Jesus preached. S.K. does use biblical references. The issue seems to be that, if human salvation is accomplished by men, it will involve only a few, and it could be entirely individual. However, if God's grace and Jesus' death accomplish the needed reform, large numbers could appropriate it. S.K.'s extreme individualism speaks more of the traditional mystic spiritual athlete of monastic life than it does of, say, St. Paul's preaching about the opening of divine grace for all. Of course, S.K. means to oppose Hegel's stress on universality and historical mass movements, but in countering Hegel he may go as far to the left as Hegel does to the right.

Christianity always needs only one, S.K. asserts, but that is true if you are speaking of Jesus and not so true if you are speaking of the masses who need spiritual release. Of course, S.K.'s aim is to force the individual to face God, whereas we all will shift our task to others or a group if we can. He wants to stress that you must involve yourself with God first, not with "the others." Yet that assumes a split between the two, whereas it could be that God is best found in loving service to the needs of others. In hastily rejecting impersonal institutional

Christianity, S.K. fails to see that it might be the way one relates to others that determines whether he can find God in church gatherings too. S.K. turned away from the human crowd with bruised feelings over his treatment, but then he makes God out to be a consoler of wounded pride, perhaps a touch too egocentric.

In place of treating people under universal classifications, S.K. thinks Christianity is unique in making the individual higher than the species. But this is lonely, and who wants to bear all the weight of facing existence alone? God never uses the people who have the gift of managing successfully with all men, unless he first confuses their lives by making them misunderstand in order to set them out alone. S.K. thinks that all the classical conversion accounts fail to describe the pain involved, and it is true that most describe conversion as a joy. S.K. thinks that to become a Christian eternally separates you from humanity, but this association of isolation with Christianity may be his most questionable and debatable thesis.

S.K. asserts that Christians are hard to tolerate, and thus they isolate themselves because they have a hatred of the world, of themselves, and of all that men have in their secular lives. If the Christian does this, then he would have to stand alone, as an individual, in isolation. Yet S.K. surely turns the Christian doctrine around here, since it speaks of love more than hatred. Perhaps it is his stress on hatred and not love which forces him to see Christianity in such isolated terms. He is sure, however, that coming close to God brings catastrophe, so it seems to be the initial shock effect he wants to describe rather than any eventual reconciliation. The initial Christian experience may be radical and alienating, but is that its end result, we must ask Kierkegaard? Only one person is needed for Christianity, S.K. is right, but this is Jesus standing alone—not the agonized individual who makes Christianity what it is all by himself.

Certainly one reason S.K. promotes such extreme individualism as necessary for Christianity is his revulsion of so much churchly stress on numbers, crowds, and the mass. He sees an alarming tendency in modern society to write for the crowd, not the strong individual, and he wants to oppose this. Human beings are corrupted by being in a crowd, and he illustrates this by saying that you, his reader, were part of the crowd who mistreated Jesus, whether you know it or not. Christian reformation, he says, is the turn against the mass, since it is each person who must be reformed. He equates the crowd with untruth, very much as Nietzsche does, but there is no evidence that these two anti-Hegelians did not reach this conclusion independently.

Jesus did not want to form a party. He wanted to be the truth related to the single individual. The Christian witness is to be involved with all men, but always individually. To be in a crowd gives a man an artificial sense of courage, but S.K.'s task is fearfully strenuous. Sartre will say this too, but S.K. has God to help him whereas Sartre does not. Christianity requires self renunciation, magnanimity, and the majority will always think this madness. What is the passage in the New Testament, S.K. asks us, which says Christianity is a point of departure for plush jobs? Christianity needs to be communicated only in a private room. The idle of the age, the tyrant, is "the mass," "the crowd." The public is a hungry monster which the public journals have to feed. In contrast, asceticism means to endorse solitary battle year after year.

God does not make public appearances, S.K. reports to us. He is present only for the single individual, never for masses. If true, this places the traditional "arguments" for God's existence in an entirely new light. We must learn not to be afraid of numbers any longer, just as a child has to learn not to be afraid of ghosts. There is a conflict between God and man. We must face it individually, not escape by some mass formula. The fall of the race today is because there are no individualists any more. Evil, he tells us, is bound up with the numerical. The agony of becoming involved with God individually is excruciating. Wars and revolutions require masses, but where getting involved with God is concerned, one single human being is enough. Adam sought to hide from God in the trees. Modern men seek a hiding place in the numeral.

Numbers change the definition of what it is to be a Christian. We human beings want to reassure ourselves with the help of large numbers, whereas S.K.'s point is to teach us what it means to stand alone and to try to force some to do it. There is no question that, with this radical reinterpretation of individuality, S.K. has provided a needed corrective for an age content with groups and mass movements. The issue is whether S.K.'s extremism is true as it stands or is simply an excess needed as the medium to discovery. And if the discovery of Christianity is an individual affair, for him to force us into this lonely position is to put us in the right condition for choice, even if the doctrine itself is not true in its radical form.

Inwardness / Communication

The writings of Saint Paul make it clear that any Christian will experience a tension between his inner and his outer life, between the flesh and the spirit. Saint Augustine made the interior way famous as the means to approach God. S.K. picks up and renews these themes in his day. He sets himself against the world of outward appearances. As the prophet of "the second reformation," S.K. takes it as his task to stress the inner or the spiritual life, its hidden and unseen qualities, and the necessity for a change in their relationship to outward form. Above all, we must realize that it is in inwardness where God can be discovered and where we can relate to him.

All of us suffer in various ways, some of which are outward, but only by the method of inner appropriation can we learn anything from these experiences (Hong & Hong, *Journals and Papers,* Vol. II, p. 460). We do not always need to show inner change by external means, which S.K. thought the medieval age tried to do with its stress on monasticism. In the first place, true inwardness is incommensurable with any external expression *(ibid.),* so that to try to mirror it outwardly is to misunderstand the essential hiddenness of the inner life. The religious man who develops his religious life must get used to the contradiction of not being able to express his inner state fully by any outward sign. The more one turns inward to develop the life of the spirit, the more he condemsn himself both to not being fully understood and to the difficulty of finding no really adequate way to express his condition to others.

Thus "inwardness" is closely connected to S.K.'s greatest problem: "communication." If it were not for the incommensurability of true inwardness, communication would be a simple matter. The result of struggling with this difficulty is S.K.'s claim that his only intended reader is "the individual" and his stress on the necessity for personal appropriation if any written work of substance is to be understood. All these factors force us to try to understand S.K.'s use of aesthetic modes of authorship to conceal a religious message. The problem is to find a way to communicate inwardness in a manner that will not be treated outwardly and thus become distorted. Little is possible by way of direct communication, for what is inward can never be conveyed as such. Yet the translation into indirect modes also places a religious message in danger of being misunderstood. There is no safe medium to which we can turn for communication in a manner safe from distortion.

Inwardness, when it exists, may be overlooked entirely, but it is also as constantly subject to distortion as it is perceived or conveyed. The one beneficial effect of such distortion is that it increases inwardness. To experience misunderstanding is to be driven more deeply into yourself and possibly also to search for God as he-alone-who-can-understand. To be able to communicate easily would tempt one to an entirely outward display. It would lure us to try to make a translation of the religious life into some overt form which is easily seen. The tension that results from this impossibility deepens the inward search. Yet, it is also true that such difficulty only increases our pressure to try to find some word or deed which can express adequately what we are experiencing inwardly.

S.K. speaks as if the eternal were experienceable only inwardly, and this gives us a hint of the qualitative difference which is latent in the inner life (ibid., p. 461). We are forced to turn from trying to seek God in the outward world, because the world around us only evidences finiteness and thus cannot disclose God. Finally, we are forced to seek God inwardly, where evidently he is not excluded for lack of space. Prayer is a natural state for persons in this situation, since experiencing inwardness should make us pray. When it is finally successful, prayer should come as a natural response. The external world is the arena where the self seeks to establish itself and to build itself up. Inwardness is the arena where the self seeks to crush itself, to become nothing before God. It is primarily within us that the encounter between God and man takes place, and this is the meaning of the life of prayer.

Only in inwardness can a new self be born; S.K. makes this clear. Outer life is characterized by change and novelty but seldom by renewal and reform. Christianity sets up the collision of inwardness with its outward expression, and it is almost the definition of the Christian life to live in this unresolvable tension. However, there is also a danger in keeping Christianity too hidden, too inward, because Christianity demands that we make the attempt to find an active expression or outlet. Nevertheless, no act can contain the Christian life or evidence it in full. Inwardness holds us back from the conceit that the performance of some outward act, some sign or ritual, can in itself be taken as the proof that one is in fact "Christian."

As S.K. reminds us on almost every page he writes, the life of a spirit bent on introspection is a strenuous task full of dread. Whenever we are forced to look into the depths of the spirit, our own or others, we learn what nothingness means. Such an experience makes us exist like the traditional hermit who has chosen to go out to fight devils alone in the desert. To be left alone to learn about oneself is a task not without its frightful aspects. If S.K. suffered, his agony took place on this inner plane and in his battle with himself, or with God. He himself constantly spoke of his outward goals: to marry, to be a country parson. Still, it is not at all out of line to view these aims as his own inadequate outward sign of what essentially was an inner and spiritual struggle.

Irony and melancholy helped S.K. to come to love inwardness (*ibid.*, p. 467). His shyness, as with many of us, can be taken as a natural cover for the inner life which demands protection and concealment. S.K. speaks of disguises, and he claims that the egotistical and frivolous aspects which others saw in him were simply a means to conceal his essentially inner directed nature. Whether or not his theatrical statements were in fact consciously contrived disguises, it is true that the development of the inner life is made easier if it is not immediately expressed but rather is protected by a different mode of outer activity. Since the inner life can be touched only indirectly, a contrasting outward lifestyle helps to point up this ironic necessity for constant indirect communication.

Yet one who comes to love God in hidden inwardness must remain prepared to renounce all if it is demanded (*ibid.,* p. 469). He can never be sure whether he can have both worlds, particularly if they come into conflict when the inner life increasingly demands to be expressed outwardly. Christianity can be held at a distance and appropriated only outwardly, but then it becomes poetry or mythology. Thus, we can properly say of the New Testament documents that they are "poetry" or "mythology," but S.K. gives us the key as to how we should understand this. Religious truths appear as myth only because we treat the documents indifferently, as objective affairs and not as matters of inward appropriation. True, the objective problems remain, for instance how to classify the Scriptures and how to reconcile any new inner experience with some appropriate outward form. Yet at least we see the problem in its true light when we recognize its essential inwardness.

S.K. is sure that God wants religion to be introduced into the middle of actual life (*ibid.,* p. 471). However, since his religion is one of inwardness, the struggle in the religious life reaches a climax over how this can be done without distortion. True, there is such a thing as "hidden inwardness" (*ibid.,* p. 472), and S.K. is sure that Christ approved of this too. There is no one form which the religious life must take either in hiding or in expressing itself, but we do know that none can be a true form unless the life involved has deepened inwardly and achieved a transformation. The origin of the struggle should stem from the inner life and not simply from the details of how to manipulate external publicity or skill in analyzing historical facts.

Of course, all of S.K.'s edifying discourses can be taken as intended to increase our inwardness. Their style often has a liturgical pattern of repetition whose intent is to deepen the reader's inner awareness. S.K.'s religious writings and commentaries on biblical themes all have a quality that induces self-reflection. In a sense, S.K.'s refusal actually to preach his sermons indicates his desire not to have them used publicly in such a way that they might be passed off as simply another ritual. The reader who will go over the words individually, S.K. thought, is more likely to learn the secret of personal appropriation than is the mere attender at public ceremonies. Preaching is too often taken as a form of direct communication, whereas the truly successful style must be indirect. It must involve the individual with himself or with God, and very little should depend on the preacher-listener relationship.

In attempting to explain his authorship by writing *The Point of View,* S.K. is forced to dwell on the notion of indirect communication, a theme which has occupied him so often. Yet oddly enough, in this work he proposes to speak out directly at last. One must be direct enough to get in touch with men, S.K. decides, and yet that opens one to misunderstanding. Of course, as long as such misunderstanding is pointed out, the aim of increasing inwardness has been served. One is forced into himself to try to solve the puzzle of how he could have been misled by appropriating the words wrongly. Since you cannot teach another the truth in any case, the closest the author—biblical or otherwise—can come is to present a puzzle. You entice your reader into a contradiction in the hope that he will be driven inward for the solution. The author becomes in fact indirect, and not direct as it may seem, because only by switching to a direct account can inwardness be fostered, due to the contradiction of using two methods and two explanations in place of one.

Of course, for S.K. the story of Abraham in his *Fear and Trembling* is the classic example of isolation and enforced inwardness. Christianity confronts man with a paradox: What is sacrificed will also be saved. He who believes what is the absurd (that both sides of the paradox are true) cuts himself off from public acceptance and is forced inward for his support. S.K.'s Knight of Faith cannot reveal himself as a knight to anyone else, and this indicates the isolation which inwardness breeds. The outer world may observe a different, even a happy man, but inwardly paradox reigns. To accept God's demands may force you to oppose the world. When this happens, if one finds the strength to do this, it will not come from outward approval. Ironically, he who lives in faith cuts himself off from others, although at the same time God demands of him actions before men which demonstrate his faith.

S.K. balances the extremity of this account of faith with the caution of his message in *Authority and Revelation*. One cannot be so private in his communication that what he expresses does not meet the norm of the founding revelation of Christianity. One must accept the burden of his isolation and the essentially inner search for God, but he must also undertake the task of finding acceptable ways to communicate his inner discoveries. Others must be able to receive these inner spiritual explorations and recognize their authenticity as Christian communication. Magister Adler, S.K.'s subject in *Authority and Revelation*, was shaken in the inwardness of emotion. Although this is necessary for the religious life, emotional upheaval does not in itself prove that it is authentically religious.

Inwardness involves dread due to the isolation it induces. *The Concept of Dread* explores the source of dread (vs. fear of an object or power). It arises in the experience of sin and the fall, plus the void which original innocence involves. However, when one realizes he has fallen from innocence, then dread over the fear of the loss of the self in nothingness also becomes an incentive to increased inwardness. And we must turn inward if we are to understand the source of the human situation. Outward behavior alone does not explain itself. The psychological observer should begin his examinations partly by trying to understand man's sense of guilt, which is difficult because it goes beyond being explained by any action or fact. This may account for why S.K. takes as his favorite biblical theme that "against God we are always in the wrong." Such a realization is the source of increased inwardness.

However, because its theme is "subjectivity," S.K.'s *Concluding Unscientific Postscript* (trans. David Swenson and Walter Lowrie, Princeton University Press, 1944) is probably the location of his longest discussion of inwardness. "Communication assumes that the subject . . . exists in the isolation of his inwardness" (*ibid.,* p. 68). The inwardness of the understanding consists in each individual coming to understand for himself. Nor is inwardness strictly associated with the religious alone: "The ethical is the inwardness of spirit" (p. 128). To be aesthetic is to live on the surface, but to face the consistency which is demanded by an ethical life is to be forced inward for additional sources of support.

"Inwardness in an existing subject culminates in passion" (p. 177). This happens because the individual seeks to manifest the truth, in spite of the fact that it remains a paradox in relation to himself as an existing individual and against the world's demands. Because God is a subject, he comes to exist only for subjectivity in inwardness, and thus he is always absent when sought outwardly. Since religious truths are always objectively uncertain, we can hold on to them only by the strength of inwardness. This indicates the crucial role S.K. assigns to inwardness in the religious life, and we realize the inner strength it requires. Truth itself is not a paradox, but its objective uncertainty makes it paradoxical when it is related to an individual who wants to appropriate it absolutely (p. 183). Thus, the passion of inwardness is a necessity if we are to hold on to truth.

Subjectively speaking, truth can exist for inwardness, which means that he who cannot achieve inwardness frustrates his only hope to appropriate truth, since no profound truth can be held onto in another way. You find no direct expression for your inwardness, and yet you must stand by it; that is true inwardness (p. 271). To exist signifies to have inwardness, since human existence finds no perfect objective expression. This also explains why we must explore every means for indirect communication. "Inwardness cannot be directly communicated" (p. 230). Direct communication shows that the orientation of the self is still outward and not inward as it should be. S.K. thought the misfortune of his age (and of every age) was to forget what inwardness is.

"Christianity is an existence-communication" (p. 538). This statement almost alone signifies the source of S.K.'s "existentialism." It is also the origin of his greatest problem as an author and as a person. Christianity is false without this depth of inwardness or subjective appropriation. There is no adequate expression for it, and yet at the same time there is a demand that it be expressed in a life and in activity as well as in words. Direct communication might make us think that Christianity's truth is a matter of words, whereas the basic problem arises because Christianity demands more than verbal expression. The real shock about the Medieval Inquisition is not so much that they burned men at the stake as that they burned them because they would not say certain words. The secret and the truth of Christianity lies only in the change it brings about in the mode of existence of the individual.

S.K.'s *Attack Upon Christendom* was written late in his life and represents the culmination of this massive paradox as he lived it out. That is, Christianity requires more than words, and yet his life was essentially that of an author. He was a writer who used words to stress subjectivity and inwardness and indirect communication. Ironically, to do this only heightens the paradox which must be lived, since Christianity must also become an "existence-communication." First there comes the drive to inwardness. Then this is followed by the drive to communicate spiritual fruits directly. But this can never be done fully. This incommensurable situation explains the essentially "driven" quality of all Christian experience—Kierkegaard's in particular.

The problem of understanding Kierkegaard, of what Christianity is, and of how an author should communicate—these three are all linked. Of course, it is the presence of the religious dimension which accentuates this, although it exists for all authorship. There is something so holy it cannot be expressed in words. If one deals with this in inwardness and is at the same time an author (or is turned into a poet), he faces problems in communication. One who knows what scholarship is should never dabble with it in the pulpit, if he understands what pulpits are for and how out of place scholarship is there. Also, suffering is still present in religious joy, and that is something difficult to express. Those who want to celebrate joy in religious services act as if suffering had ceased. They attack the very nerve of religion, although it is true that they also free themselves from a difficult task by treating worship as pure joy.

In relation to the religious, all historical presentation is a diversion, although many congregations find historical sermons just that, diverting. The religious speaker must learn what the simplest of men also know, although he may combine this with erudition if he can. Trials belong to the inwardness of religiousness, but we must never think of the author or preacher as a simple tool of communication. To be an author is a form of action, and to express inwardness in such action is a lived-through trial. Of course, your historical storytelling may be a kind of striptease to get your audience to come along, but after that it is more difficult business. Preaching is hypocrisy unless it has a close relationship to the problems of existing. To understand that you are not being understood aids communication, because it forces the person to understand himself more deeply in a way that successful stage performances never do.

Teaching is no simple task involving speaking. S.K. is convinced that the basic flaw in teaching in his age was that it left the learner's inwardness too secure. Like Socrates, S.K. would have us use puzzles and entrap the learner into a struggle. But even more difficult than teaching is the problem of how an author conveys a religious relationship to God. S.K.'s books lie before the eyes of the world, but he says he has no right to offer "explanations" which will help anyone to procure what is there at a cheaper price than he, the author, had to pay to dig them out at first. Any communication should never dare to do anything but influence others only indirectly. If anyone tries to force others to follow him, he assumes that he is the master-teacher, whereas S.K. is convinced only God has such a role.

Unless the author works indirectly, he actually becomes a hindrance to his reader, because the reader will think truth lies in accepting what is communicated to him. But this is never the case where God or the ethical life is concerned. All communication must be in the medium of imagination, and every reader is best if he preserves some naivete. The religious and the ethical life involve training or upbringing, so the author distorts the situation if he teaches as if he were simply imparting knowledge. A healthy and honest human existence must always possess an element of naivete up to the last, since otherwise it will try to grasp communication directly rather than as a child's natural response of play. We demand to understand the individual at once, whereas we must go through a few games and allow an indefinite time. Otherwise, the individual will never be known, only some universal form.

In a final subtlety, Kierkegaard says he is going to use direct communication to make his reader aware of indirect communication. He drops his mask in his later works, particularly in his self-summary of his authorship. But he indicates here that direct communication is not a simple matter. It should only make the reader aware, when he hears a matter involving the inner life explained directly, that it cannot be done. The ethical and the religious have to be communicated existentially. Thus no literary expression, direct or indirect, can communicate truth in these fields adequately. Following Socrates, S.K. agrees that strictly speaking the ethical cannot be taught. Communication here has to take the form of more than words, or perhaps we should say there is no way to convey these matters fully to another.

Ethico-religious truth can only be communicated by an I to an I, S.K. says, anticipating Martin Buber. Personality is needed. It cannot be done abstractly or by anyone. Yet God binds us to a duty to communicate what we have learned in these realms in the truest form; a hard task. S.K. reports that he has always used pseudonyms along with direct communication as a means to highlight the difficulty of the task. S.K. likes to think of himself as a teacher in the ancient style. He not only admires Socrates and quotes him, but S.K.'s use of indirect technique is quite similar to Platonic dialogue, if more radical. When things become personal, as S.K. has made them, the question immediately arises as to what it means to communicate. When matters are put on an impersonal plane, the same issue does not arise.

An author must at times set between himself and his reader "the awakening of misunderstanding." A smooth relationship between author and reader makes everything appear too easy and objective. Simplicity is to do what one says, but this state cannot be arrived at without a struggle. S.K. thinks the pastors of his time are like persons who stand on dry land and give swimming lessons. One who teaches should himself live on a religious plane, but that means also to be aware of the difficulty, if not the impossibility, of communicating religion directly. Witnessing is a form of communication, but it cannot simply be spoken out. It involves suffering. The belief and the situation of the person who offers instruction both matter if the communication is to be effective.

Indirect communication always involves sheer tension. Poetic eloquence increases in proportion to laxity. To speak as an apostle may cost you your life. To speak as a poet brings good fortune. Poetic communication takes suffering and transforms it aesthetically into a thing of beauty in which the pain is made palatable. Jesus used an indirect method and appeared as a servant. He used parable and poetry, but, as he was forced toward directness, he was also crucified. No form of writing or communication on any level of importance is easy or can be taken for granted. What the author wants to say may not be new, but, in order to have it received correctly, he may have to find a new form of expression—as Kierkegaard did.

Love/Self-denial

Love is a "very special" concept in S.K.'s thought. That is, love does not figure heavily in the philosophical writings we usually think of as defining S.K.'s distinctive work, e.g., *Concept of Dread, Fear and Trembling*. But in his edifying discourses and in the more specifically religious works, love's presence is very strong. However, just as S.K. tells us that he likes the Old Testament for its evidence of passion, and just as he uses Abraham as his religious hero, so his notion of love involves an Old Testament setting. That is, a God of love is not at all above anger and punishment and the use of harsh tests. Suffering and struggle are not incommensurate with such a God's love. The strict imposition of law and command are not outside his province. His love is hardly what we would call "romantic love," and certainly it is not pure pleasure.

In fact, as we consider S.K.'s life, suffering more than love dominates it as the defining characteristic. Or, at least we would have to say that love always finds itself enmeshed in a context of suffering. S.K.'s own love was unhappy, and his desire for love was balanced, if not overcome by, his melancholy. As S.K. presents it, love seems to characterize God's life more than man's. Or, perhaps it is best to say that if left to himself man could find some immediate form of love in his relationships. However, for the religiously disposed or the ethically inclined, the struggle of man with God and of man with himself leads first to pain and then to anguish. When finally God is discovered to be love, our nature can be discovered and the self is finally known to us too.

In any appraisal of love, *The Works of Love* (trans. David and Lillian Swenson, Princeton University Press, 1949) must of course be taken as S.K.'s major statement on what love involves. This work is a presentation of the Christian ethic and its requirements. It should answer the charge that S.K. either ignores ethical codes in his stress on subjectivity or that he is so uncertain as to whether he is a Christian that he cannot settle down and lead that life. *Works of Love* is the assured statement of one speaking as a Christian to other Christians. Furthermore, it gives little evidence of being involved in the tumult of S.K.'s life. It seems to spring from a deeper level of spiritual reflection, just as his edifying discourses do. This is evidence that S.K. knew the spiritual repose of religious belief as well as the turmoil which he publicized so loudly. The religious life does involve both ethical commitment and individual struggle, but S.K. also knows a God of calm injunction as well as one of paradoxical confrontation.

In the Forword S.K. speaks of his writings on love as "Christian meditations." Indeed, they embody a deep reflective and liturgical quality in tone and in cadence. He draws an important distinction, which is the theme of the work, that because they are "Christian" these meditations are about the *works* of love and not simply about love itself. This strikes a note of importance in S.K.'s life and writing, because as time goes on, he becomes increasingly concerned about what it means for a Christian to stand as a "witness to the truth." Furthermore, as a writer he eventually is overcome by the fact that a Christian life must involve more than words, that it demands action and commitment by the person. Dread forces each "knight of faith" into internal isolation, but love urges the Christian to recognize his or her need to communicate the works of love.

In the prayer with which S.K. opens the book, he strikes the theme common to his religious meditations, that God is a God of love and that as such he is the source of love. This of course is similar to traditional Platonic and Augustinian doctrines, that is, one moves from an experience of the love of the good on to see God as its primary example or form. As he stands before God, S.K. also reports his most common experience before the divine, the feeling of being "without claim or merit." This conviction stands in interesting contrast to S.K.'s repeated reference to himself as a genius, or as competing with geniuses. Before men, he is prone to complain of not being sufficiently recognized for his rightness. But where God is concerned, he shows the traditional humility of piety and stands quietly without the fuss of virtuous self-assertion.

Chapter I starts with the theme of the hidden life of love (p. 5). Love cannot be seen, and therefore it is chief among those things which are not visible. Thus, to trust in love involves a belief in the reality of things unseen. He who will not venture to risk deception cuts himself off from love, because it is always possible to be mistaken about something which remains essentially unseen. The man who thinks he is shrewd, and who will not gamble on love, only works himself out of the rewards of love through his cleverness. Deception is always possible—the cautious man is right. However, what cannot be seen can be recognized by indirection in its fruits. One can be deceived about love, but love may also be the only thing to endure when deception is gone. Love requires the ultimate in human adventure and commitment.

An unwillingness to venture, plus a desire to be safe, holds one back from love. Such reluctance stems from the conceit that one can rely upon himself and thus need take no such risks. A self-confident person can give sympathy to those who need it, but his consolation lacks love. He will not bend himself that far. Love is a secret, so that he who rejects what remains secret also rejects love. However, love is simply the epitome of all forms of life which remain essentially hidden and can only be revealed in other ways. "The life of thought is hidden, its expressions in speech is its revelation" (p. 7). Thus, viewing love as a secret life is not so strange but actually is a test case for how we understand all human existence. There are forms for life's expression (e.g., art, religion, ceremony), but its sources are not equally visible. Where the self is concerned, we must always deal in indirection.

The mysterious origin of love, however, is grounded in the love of God, and so love has an unfathomable connection with the whole of existence. It is this mysterious origin which prevents you from seeing love's source, which is another reason we are forced to venture where love is concerned. However, the paradoxical quality present is that love can be known by its fruits. That is, its actions and results are seen while its origins, its nature in itself, is not. Of course, words and verbalizing are often love's only evidence. If so, we know that this is an immature and deceptive love (p. 10). As a man who himself has poured out volumes of print, S.K. is sensitive to those aspects of life which must go beyond verbal expression or else become false.

No word can be used to prove love's genuineness, nor in the strictest sense can any act in itself prove that love is not a passing fancy. Charity can be administered in an unkind and in a selfish way. It is not so much the action itself but the hidden intent of the performer that is in question. We want to know *how* the word is spoken or the action intended. Yet since love itself remains unseen, one also wants to guard himself or herself against deception. In doing this we may withhold love, whereas S.K. wants to suggest that "the best defense against hypocrisy is love" (p. 13).

Like can be known only by like, so that only he who is willing precariously to commit himself to love can hope to be able to recognize love in another. Love has a quality which makes it abide. If one persists in his own offer of love to others, this love and its recognition in others may outlast the uncertainties and deceptions involved. All this is interesting and insightful regarding love, but it does not involve the paradox which becomes S.K.'s focal point: That in Christianity love is "commanded" as a duty. If love were something easy to determine, it would make more sense to command it, since its execution could be observed. But how can we command something which is never seen?

Faith involves a paradox for the knight of faith due to the incommensurability of the notion that the divine has become human, the infinite finite. Love is less a matter of torment, but still it involves its own paradox for the Christian. That is, action which can never be directly observed is demanded of him under the injunction of a divine command. In love God's softer side is united with his harsher side, the demand for unconditional obedience. We expect dread to involve paradoxical aspects, but, in a simpleminded fashion, we at first expect love to be easy and pure. Among men it probably never is so, but love as we find it in God clearly discloses its paradoxical link with God's command of what essentially cannot be commanded.

Of course, in biblical terms this comes to us in the Christian injunction that one should love his neighbor as himself. Christians have been tangled for years in the puzzle of trying to fill in the formula of who is a "neighbor." "Neighbor" has usually been broadly defined as anyone, but then the command to love so indiscriminately becomes all the more puzzling. Christian love is distinctive in its apparent contradiction: that loving, which cannot be forced, has become a duty and is extended to all, not just the chosen.

This, S.K. is convinced, is the core of Christianity's novelty, and it is what shocks and astonishes the pagan. The pagan is now defined as one who thinks that love is voluntary, and this designation belongs primarily to those who assume they can choose how to direct love's attention. The Christian ought never to accept too easily the injunction to love his neighbor, for this demand goes against the natural grain of man, and it always will. The novelty of the command never wears off, and its shocking aspects never grow dull. Thus, heathendom is always present, and Christianity can never take over as the sole advocate for what is good. One always lapses into the pagan view of love, and then we need to be shocked back into remembering the constant newness of the Christian proposal. It can neither grow old nor be taken for granted.

Love makes a man secretive, and thus it is linked with faith (p. 24). Love even becomes a symbol of faith in its secretiveness. This notion is a quite different and in a sense a more interesting symbol than Abraham's unconditional willingness to obey God's command to sacrifice Isaac as S.K. presents faith in *Fear and Trembling*. The teleological suspension of the ethical is one thing; the private life of love is quite another. And love forces no violation of the ethical, even though one stands alone. In fact, love may conform to ethical requirements; it is just that such conformity is in itself no proof of love. Yet love when taken as a duty has certain advantages: It becomes secure and is no longer dependent on the flux of human feeling. Duty, S.K. is convinced, drives anxiety out and makes love secure. This is true only in its basic impulse and not in its fulfillment, since each new act of love is a novelty.

By way of contrast, there is such a thing as immediate love, but it is subject to flux and all too easily becomes hate or jealousy (p. 29). Therefore, if we obey the command to love, this changes love. It eliminates jealousy by making love a duty. Although one would not ordinarily think of the changed nature of immediate love as constituting freedom, love accepted as a duty does become "free" in the sense of being free from change. One who admits his necessity to love becomes free in that he is open to accept his own need. One who does this can release himself and then feel free in his love. The issue is one of momentary freedom vs. long-term release: "Immediate love makes a man free in one moment, and in the next moment dependent" (p. 32).

Despair once again enters into S.K.'s considerations as it did in *Sickness Unto Death.* Yet where love is concerned he offers us the possibility of becoming secure against despair. Love alone cannot accomplish that since it is subject to too violent changes, but love when accepted as a duty can become secure. When immediate love changes, it becomes unhappy and falls into despair over its inability to sustain itself. On the other hand, despair is driven out when God supports love by commanding it. If modern marriages are based on immediate love, this might explain our high divorce rate, as love shifts quixotically. Like the personality who covers up his despair but nevertheless is in despair deeply without knowing it, immediate love shows that it concealed despair earlier by falling into it later as time changes the situation. Such happiness is a desperate happiness and so is easily subject to change. "Despair is a disproportion in his inmost being" (p. 34). The shifts in love and happiness do not cause this; they only reveal it.

S.K. wants the Christian to understand everything differently from the non-Christian, and this acceptance of love as a duty is the Christian's most distinctive mark. Yet you cannot say to anyone who calls himself a Christian that he is not one. The origins of his love, which determine this, always remain hidden from man's inspection and so close off all final human judgment.

Augustine defined men by the *direction* their love takes, that is whether love is directed primarily toward God or toward creatures. S.K. prefers to divide men according to the *source* of their love, and this provides an intersting contrast to the famous Augustinian criterion for the division between the two cities, one of man and one of God. Christianity's essential form is self-abnegation. The source of love determines whether this is a selfish concern or is more self-denying than that. In this context, S.K. uses love as the test of whether you are Christian, rather than demanding the much more strenuous effort outlined in *Fear and Trembling* (p. 302). He ends *The Works of Love* with a note on God's grace as it is manifested in love when properly understood (see the Retrospective Summary). This indicates that "love" functions for S.K. much like the traditional theological concept of "grace."

Although love is a minor note in S.K.'s writing as a whole, it still is a pervasive theme, and upon examination it proves to be ever present beneath the surface of his thought. Even in the harsh tone of *Attack Upon Christendom,* with its stress on the necessity of martyrdom as the only true Christian way, love appears. But now it is the love of a passion that refuses to see something it prizes treated easily and lightly. *Authority and Revelation* is also a strident book in its denunciation of the validity of any claim to private revelation. Nevertheless, love appears there too as the emotion of falling in love is equated with Christian reawakening. However, a love like this needs the firmness of traditional Christian concepts for its valid expression.

One may be deeply affected, as S.K. admitted the crazy pastor who came to him, Magister Adler, was. Yet God's revelation is something not produced by the individual; it is given to him. We would expect love to be discussed in S.K.'s *Christian Discourses,* where he defines the Christian task as "loving God" and "loving much" (see "All things work together for good—if we love God" and his closing prayer on the sinner). However, it is interesting to see that love also appears, where we might least expect it, in *The Concept of Dread* (trans. Walter Lowrie, Princeton University Press, 1946). Poets associate love with an element of dread (p. 64), and the triumph of love is pictured as that which transfigures the spirit and drives out dread (p. 72).

Just as love is still present in S.K.'s noisy concluding *Attack,* so it is on his mind from the beginning. In his first work, *The Concept of Irony* (trans. Lee M. Capel, New York: Harper & Row, 1965), he links love to Socrates and to irony, since "Irony is the negative of love" (p. ii). Love is pictured as the medium of Socratic teaching (p. 213). We think of his *Fear and Trembling* as analyzing and recommending emotions other than love to the would-be believer, but it is clear that what drives one to the summit of faith, to that isolation and paradox, ultimately can only be the love of God. However, it becomes clear that love is never simple. It is Abraham's love of his son, Isaac, which brings the stringent test of faith upon him. It is love that forces Abraham to choose between his fatherly love and the love of God which commands him to obey even in the face of absurdity. If love did not complicate life, the fear and trembling of faith would never be encountered in the first place.

Of course, *Either/Or* links love to the aesthetic life, but deeper than that love is a constant subject which forms the substructure of the aesthetic and ethical life. In fact, love provides S.K. with so much example and subject matter for his writing that one is forced to wonder if his autobiographical claim is not right. Did his own unhappy love affair turn him into an author who wrote out his love on paper, becoming a lover in secret rather than in fact?

S.K.'s inability to marry makes love his constant topic, and his love of God is the source and driving power of his religious torment. He may argue with God, but it is his pervasive love of God which constantly inspires the divine-human conversation. Love drives him to write in frustration, just as love drives him to approach God directly when his formal and institutionally-mediated religious life is not satisfactory. In fact, one wonders if love is not for S.K. the basic question. You are in love with God whether you know it consciously or not—that is the paradoxical condition of the religious life. Furthermore, this is a love which tends to block out other attachments. Thus, it may be as much the source of S.K.'s broken engagement as the melancholy he blames more openly.

Love is the aesthetic side of life, but the way in which S.K. makes marriage into a symbol indicates how love leads to something ethical and even religious. Love must constantly be referred to God, even in marriage. In Christianity love finds that it must suffer many fates in order to prove itself, e.g., crucifixion. Love is the source of happiness, but it is also very serious business. In seeking immediacy as it does, love always leads beyond itself to the heart of the serious problems in life and in religion. In *Thoughts on Crucial Situations* (trans. David Swenson, Minneapolis: Augsburg, 1941) love is portrayed as "mysterious" (p. 43), so that love shares all of the difficult characteristics involved in understanding God's nature. Love does conquer all, but it also leads us to the heart of God's mystery. Love therefore is both revealing and the ultimate source of mystery.

The marriage ceremony invites lovers, not to a victory celebration, but essentially to a struggle. Youthful enthusiasm will disappear as life's serious decisions are required, and it should then become evident that it is oneself that needs changing more than the world. Love needs resolution to survive more than it needs happiness (p. 67). Love is happiness and the source of happiness, but it is also paradoxically present at the heart of every crucial situation in life.

In *For Self-Examination* (trans. Walter Lowrie, Princeton University Press, 1944) love is connected not unexpectedly with the movement of spirit and with hope. The Holy Spirit brings hope and it also brings love. This connects love to grace as essentially something given by God. God is unchanging love (p. 14), but this fact is as frightening to man in its judgment of his changeableness as it is comforting. Love, of course, hides a multitude of sins (pp. 18–23). This favorite statement of S.K.'s indicates how love operates in his thought as his counterpart to the theological doctrine of "grace," which he is sometimes said to overlook. The one to whom little has been given loves little (p. 9). The Christian has received much he has not earned and thus he is open to love much. God's word is portrayed as a precious letter from a lover (p. 51).

Love can also be one of "the strongest and deepest expressions of selfishness" (p. 97). It is precisely this difficulty which the love of God hopes to transform, and this change is what the Christian calls "conversion." *Stages on Life's Way* (trans. Walter Lowrie, New York: Shocken Books, 1967) begins with S.K.'s version of the Socratic "Banquet Scene." S.K. borrows from his philosophical model, Socrates, the centrality of love as a subject of discourse. Love may seem to disappear when God appears (p. 105), but it is precisely the Christian discovery that, when erotic love has fled, all love is not absent. It is still present as transformed by God. Thus, S.K.'s life and works are not misunderstood if they are taken as the diary of his sometimes violent, sometimes enlightening, love affair with God.

In his *Journals* S.K. actually remarks that love, not fear and trembling, is the prime mover of the Christian life, which is quite a different notion from the popular opinion about S.K. But he does not want to confuse this with self-love, which is sheer egoism, unless it is also love for God which transforms it into love for all. S.K. even treats the difficulty in our understanding God's incarnation as a difficulty in love, not in a logical incommensurability between eternal and temporal as we often think of S.K.'s view. Instead, the paradox of love is that one so high (God) should make himself comprehensible to one of low position in the equality of love. It is love, not so much infinity, that forms the core of the paradox man faces in the divine nature. If we can resolve this, man actually learns from God what love is, something he cannot do from another human being.

Love becomes self-denial, but only if it is rooted in the relationship to God. If people complain about being lonely and get married, they call this love, but it is really self-love. Also, when a person loves his friend, it is by no means clear that he loves God. But when a person loves his enemy, it is clear that he fears and loves God. Faith is only known by love, S.K. tells us. This does not remove the mystery of love, but at least it gives us a better chance to experience faith than the paradox of *Fear and Trembling*. It is audacious for man to venture to love God, but it is also necessary. However, from a Christian point of view, to love God, and also to want to be happy and fortunate in the world at the same time, are not possible together. S.K. again inserts suffering into love, as he has inserted it in every human relationship.

Yet S.K. adopts a more radical view of God's nature at this point: God wants to be loved. To love God is to be a Christian—a different and simpler definition of Christianity than S.K. has often given us. That God is love means that he will do everything to help you love him, that is, to be transformed into likeness to him. Christianity begins in the transition to love God or to be remade into likeness with God. But humanly speaking, God must first make you unhappy if he is to love you and you are to love him. S.K. does not leave love in simple terms. He ties it to the demand for self-denial, which keeps love constantly complex and never a state simply to be enjoyed. The meaning of suffering is to die to immediacy, but love needs immediacy and so it must struggle against suffering.

Love related to God requires self denial, as S.K. has stressed before. This means suffering may not be so antithetical to love as it seems, for love must become detached from self-love, and suffering can be an instrument to accomplish this, although it does not happen necessarily. Some who suffer become more intensely selfish. Christianity requires surrender of earthly things, but it wants this to be voluntary, not forced. A little adversity can help one die to the world, but only if the adversity is imposed out of love. Somehow a man or woman must be brought closer to the edge of suffering and misery to get the actual taste of Christianity. But no suffering can compel a man to die to the world. That must be done freely, since increased selfishness is also a possible result of suffering. S.K. goes on to say that loving God involves hating oneself, but that statement may go too far, and we must treat it as one of his characteristic over-statements.

Melancholy/Humor

It is "melancholy," S.K. tells us, which prevented him from marrying as was his heart's desire. And surely melancholy was partly responsible for making him into a poet. Since the "poetic" is an indirect means of communication, melancholy is also linked with S.K.'s problem of how best to establish communication between individuals. It is also involved in the relationship between the author and his work, since we must understand his mood in order to understand the writing.

If melancholy involves a depression of spirits, a gloomy mood or condition, we can understand why S.K. is so often referred to as the "melancholy Dane." He is pensive and moody in print. He is quietly serious in his thought. He is also irascible. To understand why this is so is to form a catalogue of the problems which S.K. faced. It is also to discover why he took each one as his own challenge. S.K. had reason to be sad or dejected at times in his professional as well as in his private life. Of course, all this refers to his inner state more than to his outward condition. If he was inwardly gloomy, this was not always evident to the public, except near the end of his life when he spoke less indirectly.

His melancholy is perhaps derived from this irreconcilable discrepancy between the inner and outer condition, the public versus the private situation, rather than from any strictly internal source. The inner can neither become the outer nor can it be communicated directly, S.K. was convinced. This drives either the poet or the religious personality into an enforced isolation which can never be fully overcome, not even by becoming an author and explaining it in print. If S.K. was somewhat odd in his physical appearance, it is still true that his childhood and public life were outwardly successful. His torment over the revelation of his father's religious doubts and private scandalous behavior gave him an incentive to gloomy introspection. However, S.K. was firmly established as a celebrity with the church and the government, as well as being financially secure and well cared for.

The disclosure of his inner torment came as a surprise to many who knew him, so that his particular form of melancholy tends to be an inner state concealed from the external world. Likewise, his gloom about the state of religion in Denmark stands in contrast to the apparently popular and well supported clergy of the time. S.K.'s inability to become outwardly what he would like to be (husband, country parson) is as much the cause of his melancholy as it is the source of his frustration. "Remorse," which S.K. stresses so often as being necessary for the religious life (e.g., in *Purity of Heart*), is also linked to melancholy. Anyone who lives without a gulf between his inner and outer condition is not likely to understand remorse. The entirely happy man is not a serious candidate to be religiously affected, and much of S.K.'s sensitivity on religious affairs must be attributed to his brooding inner nature.

In his *Journals* S.K. claims that he is without the expectation of leading a happy earthly life (1836–37). Yet, looking at the comfort of his external situation, we must conclude that the source of his unhappiness is primarily inner. It stems largely from his melancholy mood, but what causes that mood? What problems, when they are reflected upon, induce it? S.K. often speaks of his unusual intellectual powers. To be condemned to lead only an intellectual mode of existence—this itself is a cause for melancholy. As the father of "existentialism," S.K. demands a life filled with more than dialectical thought. His growing conviction about religion drives him to witness it by action. We can understand his desire to be a country parson and his gloom over not becoming one. It indicates his inability to move from thought to deed. The moods which S.K. records are the extremes of romantic depression and exultation. He is capable of both great heights and great depths of feeling. Such an inability to be moderate is bound to cause melancholy. Yet the issues which S.K. treats almost require these extremes of feeling, if they are not to be taken too lightly.

Truth for S.K. is not found in the daily routine, nor can it be read off the surface of life as such. Some depth of feeling and inner turmoil is necessary if any penetration into truth is to be achieved. A calm soul can hardly grasp or sustain what by its nature cannot be held without intense effort, that is, truth. S.K. says his era needs passion. But paradox produces pathos as well as passion, and it is irreconcilable paradox which causes the self to experience melancholy. His abortive engagement to Regine Olsen represents for S.K. his attempt to overcome his melancholy. His breaking that engagement signifies for him the fact that one's inner situation cannot change as easily as the outer. It continues to exist as the source of that which will make him into an author. Melancholy, S.K. believes, cannot be shared or overcome. It must simply be borne alone. Ironically, however, his writing may be taken as his attempt to share his melancholy with his reader.

S.K. is caught between understanding and misunderstanding. He reports many times his conviction that no one can understand him. At the same time *The Point of View* is his own attempt to achieve a complete understanding for his work. As long as he remains silent and a pseudonymous author, he is open to be misunderstood by his use of indirection. However, when he speaks out at the end of his life as he does, he says he is doing so to set the record straight. The question is whether justifying himself achieves genuine understanding or only increases confusion.

Melancholy itself demands heroic efforts to overcome its self-inflicted isolation, and yet in its nature it cannot cease to be. S.K.'s preoccupation in later life with the questions of becoming a "witness" and a "martyr" is the kind of self-persecution which melancholy seems to inflict on those who bear it. The origin of melancholy is a disproportion between soul and body, but it also stems from the conflict between the aesthetical, the ethical, and the religious in life. One becomes melancholy over his inability ever to communicate truth directly—except to an individual privately.

S.K.'s ideal to marry and to become a priest stands in contrast to the reality of his bachelor style and his secular life. They are as much the source of his melancholy and authorship as they are its results.

His melancholy made him prefer to be looked on as mad rather than work hard enough to be properly understood. One is melancholy because he understands that there are things which cannot be understood and because no significant truth can ever be given directly to another. The "individual" is S.K.'s favorite category, and yet to lead an isolated and individual life is to be doomed to live in melancholy. The only outward evidence one can give is a poetic expression in authorship. If God is to be approached inwardly, and if our primary need is for inward renewal, no external act can ever accomplish this. Each one is left to himself.

These inner explorations eventually produce a change in S.K.'s public or outer performance. But until the time he finds a way to speak out in 1848, melancholy is his daily silent companion. His age prefers the immediate or the aesthetic in its expression, and those modes are the only road to happiness. Thus, he is doomed to be reflective in such an outer-oriented time, and this places him in the depth of melancholy by not being able to share in the spirit of the day. Yet, S.K. was able to be happy about his unhappiness, which is one sign of a melancholy nature. It provided a fresh understanding of Christianity and the new reformation it needed. S.K.'s melancholy is associated with his religious feeling, but it requires him to live out his personal existence on a different plane from his work.

Yet melancholy is also an inestimable blessing, due to the insight it brings and the spur to productivity it offers. S.K. is different from other men, and he knows he can never be the same as others. This provides his source of inner suffering, and it supplies his impetus to authorship, as an attempt both to express melancholy and to overcome it. To love God is to suffer and to struggle to find a way to express that suffering externally, that is, to overcome it in commitment.

The theme of melancholy emerges in so much of S.K.'s writings that we must believe him when he says: "melancholy also is something real which one does not obliterate with a stroke of the pen" (*Stages on Life's Way,* trans. Walter Lowrie, New York: Shocken Books, 1967, p. 171). It makes one unable to join in the joy of life as he imagines others do, and so any joy which comes he carries as a double burden. He is related to life in an unreal way. He has only an abstract notion of what makes life joyful and happy for others, because he cannot enter into it himself. S.K. could put on his disguise, go out in public and apparently put off his melancholy, but still he reports that it merely "waits for me when I am alone" (p. 189). Nevertheless, this experience can also be positive: "From the bitterness of melancholy is distilled a vital joy, a sympathy, a heartiness, which certainly cannot embitter the life of any person" *(ibid.)*. Melancholy is not pleasant to live in, but it has much to offer.

In melancholy one feels inwardly dejected, but it is also the source of strength when danger comes that must be met (p. 249), because it enables you to stand alone. Melancholy, just as much as faith, isolates the individual. It makes it impossible for him to have any confidant (p. 342), and this perhaps is part of the reason S.K. is driven toward God. Melancholy searches for the dreadful. Possibly this is what lies at the root of S.K.'s sensitivity which produced *The Concept of Dread.* Since religiously one must be responsive to the terrible, melancholy is also religiously useful. One thinks of marriage and companionship as disposing of melancholy, but it does not. Its roots are deeper and it is not so easily driven out. "Melancholy is the condensation of possibility" (p. 385), and as such it is rooted in the world and in the reflective man's perception of existence.

In a sense melancholy actually serves as S.K.'s confidant. "My melancholy is the most faithful mistress I have known, what wonder, then, that I love in return" (*Either/Or,* trans. David and Lillian Swenson, Oxford University Press, 1946, Vol. I, p. 16). Yet his despair is also derived from this tendency to melancholy (p. I-115), so that it can never be an entirely happy love affair. To have a strong imagination is to experience melancholy over the disparity between the real and the possible. To be inventive is inevitably to know melancholy. The only way to overcome this inner discrepancy is, in the Socratic phrase, "to choose oneself." S.K. sees melancholy as the defect of his age, since it deprives one of the "courage to command, of courage to obey, of power to act, of the confidence necessary to hope" (p. II-20). In this respect, melancholy is at once a block to the religious life as well as the source of our sensitivity to it. This psychological paradox inhibits action.

Whoever possesses it is bound by the chain of melancholy, because it is connected to the only state that begets dread in the apprehension of freedom and possibility. Melancholy holds one back from escaping dread, although writing offers a release and can repress melancholy temporarily. Nevertheless, gradually S.K.'s nature changed, until it reached the point where he could drop his use of pseudonyms and speak openly. His reserve was lost and he was finally able to release the burden of his melancholy. However, this did not come until the end of his authorship, after the poetic-reflective distance caused by melancholy had produced his expressive and rapid volume of work. Intellect, melancholy, and memory developed the self-torturing torments of his heart and were overcome late in life.

S.K. is a reflective individual in an age which is spontaneous and immediate, and that produces profound melancholy *Armed Neutrality and An Open Letter* (trans. Howard & Edna Hong, New York: Simon and Schuster, 1968, p. 62). Sin and dissipation can cover this over for awhile, but that makes one feel almost more deranged and guilty. He struggled and he suffered fearfully, S.K. tells us (p. 85). Through Christ he dared to believe he could be saved from this (p. 88). In some sense he did finally break into openness after struggling with himself in the way faith must be achieved inwardly. S.K. never claims to be a saint in his suffering, only a penitent (p. 97). Yet melancholy invents deception, and this explains why he can be thought to be the most frivolous of all men in his day. Just as it arises from the disproportion between inner and outer life, so melancholy prevents us from ever perfectly expressing the one through the other.

Melancholy must be the catalyst needed to open the way for an exploration of psychological states. *Repetition,* S.K.'s first major "experiment in psychology" (trans. Walter Lowrie, New York: Harper & Row, 1964), draws upon this experience heavily. It is melancholy that drives the lover whom S.K. reports on in this book, and it opens the way for his love of recollection (p. 39). Because melancholy induces loss, it allows us to understand the necessity of repetition. One's life is in a sense over in the first instant and then it must be recollected. This realization stirs a sense of melancholy, since melancholy reflects on loss. However, repetition and the strength to will repetition is the only way to transform an absorption with death and overcome melancholy with a healthy outlook. Evidently the power called for in repetition would neither be needed nor recognized if it were not for melancholy.

Melancholy works against involvement, and so it humiliates what S.K. calls the "feminine art" of drawing one into relationship (p. 89). Yet strangely, melancholy also induces sympathy and can even cause one to think he is in love out of sympathy (p. 90). Hearing S.K. say this, one wonders how much it might have had to do with S.K.'s own "falling in love." Could this be the source of his constant preoccupation with love affairs in his writing? S.K. thinks melancholy is only attractive to women and is an advantage to them (p. 91), but this is true only if it is experienced from a distance. It is never pleasant to live with. Thus, it is clear that melancholy is a two-edged sword. It attracts and induces relationships through increased sympathy. But at the same time, it is that which isolates and forces one away from others. S.K. surely spent his life in just such an alternation between reaching out and reaching in.

As we should suspect, when S.K. comes to account for his authorship in *The Point of View,* (trans. Walter Lowrie, London: Oxford University Press, 1939) he is forced to account for his melancholy also. Furthermore, in considering how to become a contemporary disciple of Jesus, one must understand himself as well as the issue at hand. That is, he must if he is to have any hope to achieve commitment where Christianity is concerned. Truth is involved in melancholy, since no appropriation of truth can be achieved until the origin and texture of psychological moods are understood. We have to learn to move in relation to the demand of moods if we are to expand our perception.

S.K.'s attack upon the established Danish state church late in his life stems from his melancholy and his attempt to overcome it. The dark mood of melancholy draws one inward, and S.K. spent his early professional life in this way. But melancholy also leads to the desire for escape, so that finally S.K. discovers his personal key to release in the notion of "witness." S.K. struggles to find the proper outer expression for his inward feeling, but he is never able to do this in his professional life. To "witness" means to stand out from the crowd, and in analyzing that notion S.K. discovers what must lie behind it if any witness is to be genuine. Martyrdom cracks the isolation of faith and makes what is internal external. One must stand out, although one must stand out alone. There is not as much time for melancholy when you are under attack. Nevertheless, it is still there even if it is covered over in the excitement.

The inner revolution in religion, which S.K. thought of himself as inducing, is not unconnected with melancholy. When one is busy with reform, as he thought Luther was, there is little time for internal restructuring. But if you consider the outward calm of S. K.'s life and times, the religious pressure of melancholy must express itself elsewhere. First it is driven inward to induce basic personal change, and next it gathers itself for some new external proposed reform. Nothing external is sufficient to induce internal revolution. Only by stirring up sympathy for suffering can we gain sufficient strength to bring the novelty we want into existence. Ironically, such reform itself remains unseen largely because it is internal and thus still subject to test by its orthodox consequences.

If melancholy provides S.K. with the key to the exploration of both psychological mood and inner religious life, no one can understand either himself or Christianity as long as he remains totally in a happy mood. This is why S.K.'s understanding of Christianity is essentially connected with dread. Happiness covers over the soul's disproportion, and S.K. recommends that we experience the heaviness of repentance and remorse. Only that laborious way really teaches us much about the psychological landscape. If he were not born melancholy, S.K. would have had to become so if he wanted to be an author over against the demands of his pleasure dominated times. His aesthetic works evidence a light touch and a sense of humor which he never quite loses, but it is melancholy which deepens his religious mood.

Consider the difficulties involved in forming a true self. It is a hard task, and an authentic self is never a thing given to us. If you do realize this self-formation, it is no wonder that melancholy is natural, because the self must constantly sustain itself between possibility and necessity. The loss of the self is easy, and its loss so often goes unnoticed beneath the surface of a life which remains unchanged. Melancholy is a consequent mood whenever one tries to discover how the self can be sustained. In any single moment you can find identity, but melancholy is deepseated. We would like to possess our life securely and with necessity, but it can only be captured in a moment. The task of constituting the self keeps melancholy continually waiting outside the moment of decision. It lurks in the knowledge that another definite choice lies always before us.

S.K. contrasts humor to irony, both of which are as important to him as melancholy, although it does not always appear so. All three moods are contingent on one's not having compromised with the world, so that he who gives in and lets his decision be made for him may apparently avoid melancholy, but his sense of irony and humor will be dulled. Christianity actually has a certain humorous content which one must appreciate. It declares that truth is hidden in the mystery. And given the philosophers' lust to acquire truth directly, Christianity places them in a slightly humorous situation. It also leads men to regard worldly wisdom humorously, which will infuriate those who take secular sophistication seriously. We see the humorous in Christianity in Jesus' statement, "My yoke is easy and my burden is light." To be a Christian in the world is extremely heavy, and it is heavy because it requires self-denial.

Although S.K. usually is more likely to find dread in Christianity, he does say that humor appears in Christ's utterances. With the addition of a polemical cast, they would be humorous, but in Jesus' mouth they actually become redeeming. Irony can produce a certain tranquility, which Jesus imparts. The Christian humorist is like a plant of which only the roots are visible but whose flower unfolds for a loftier sun. But S.K. is sure the humorist can never become a systematizer. The systematizer believes he can say everything and that whatever cannot be said is erroneous and secondary. But the Christian is a humorist precisely because he believes truth is hidden in a mystery, and this prevents him from becoming a systematizer qua Christian.

The humorous expression for becoming a Christian is "weakness," because it appears that way. But humor is also the joy which has overcome the world, and that is the central experience of Christianity. However, humor by definition becomes a polemical factor in the Christian view of life, due to the necessity imposed on us to spread the gospel. The comic is always based on a contradiction, and Christianity contains quite a few of them—overcoming power by weakness, loving one's enemies, etc. Eternity is too earnest a place to allow laughter, but Kierkegaard hopes there will be an intermediate place where one will be permitted to laugh outright. He is sure he will find pious pagans, like Socrates, in such a place. We need such an intermediate heaven for those who up until then have been too tense and concerned in the pursuit of truth to laugh.

If weeping is a divine invention and laughter is the devil's, then the world naturally tends toward the comic. Judgment in this world is so harsh that in the next world it would be nice to look forward to witty judgments. Christianity is not God's irony over man, because we have the power to transform Christianity into irony. And S.K. is convinced that his entire existence is really the deepest irony. The whole existence of Socrates, he tells us, is and was irony, and S.K. likes to model his role in life on Socrates. We think of S.K. primarily in terms of melancholy, because he stresses it, but humor, irony, and the comic play a greater role in his life and thought than is at first evident.

Midwife/Teacher

Like so many proponents of a philosophical revolution, Søren Kierkegaard continually harks back to Socrates and to the Socratic spirit of inquiry. Socrates is one of the figures he mentions most often, and it is Socrates who forms the base of Kierkegaard's Master's thesis, *The Concept of Irony*. It has, as S.K. says, a "constant reference to Socrates" (trans. Lee M. Capel, New York: Harper & Row, 1965). Irony comes to play a large role in S.K.'s own relation to philosophy, to religion, and to life, but he learned its function first from Socrates. Kierkegaard obviously read Plato extensively, and perhaps this gave him his wedge to break away from Hegel. Socrates appears many times in S.K.'s most important systematic work, *The Concluding Unscientific Postscript*. Thus, Socrates must also have something to do with forming Kierkegaard's notion of "subjective truth" as he later expounds it.

The concept of the teacher as "midwife" appears in S.K.'s most extensive treatment of the student-teacher relationship, "A Project of Thought" in *Philosophical Fragments* (trans. David Swenson and Howard Hong, Princeton University Press, 1962, pp. 11–37). According to S.K., one who instructs should serve only as the midwife who brings another's ideas to birth. Nevertheless, S.K. goes further and makes a radical advance on Socrates; he claims that the knowledge awakened was not eternally latent in the learner. It does not lie there simply waiting to be brought forth. Instead, the one who desires to relieve his ignorance does not even know what he wants or needs to ask. The learner can not simply recollect his former knowledge, as

Socrates indicates, in order to cure his ignorance. He simply is in no position to recognize the truth. He first needs a fundamental reorientation. Only God can accomplish such a new birth, so that God becomes the midwife of all fundamental change in human understanding (p. 38). It is he with whom the learner argues. To struggle with God is to open oneself to potential fundamental change.

Although it is perhaps most prominent in the *Philosophical Fragments,* the theme of the teacher appears and reappears in all of Søren Kierkegaard's written work. Although S.K. became neither husband nor pastor nor teacher in a formal sense, his life and writing are still marked by these recurring themes. S.K. did teach and still does, although his lessons were learned better by a later generation than his own. Kierkegaard's writing style, his stress on the individual and on indirect communication, are all attempts to teach. He had much to say to his generation, but he knew that the problem was how to communicate it so that the lesson could be learned. We know from his veneration of Socrates that the teacher serves only as an instrument, but for S.K. the learner does not have the knowledge latent in him, as the Socratic notion of recollection from an earlier life had suggested.

The problem for the teacher, then, is that the pupil is not in a position to learn, and he cannot be taught en masse but only as a single individual. The generation has a lesson it needs to learn, but it cannot be communicated on a mass level. The effort of the teacher, then, goes more toward attempting to put the hearer in the position to learn. The listener cannot be forced, but the teacher can perhaps bring him in to the right position. If he can be made to realize his error and his radical distance from truth, the teacher may induce the student to search. The teacher excites the quest more than he controls the result.

In terms of Søren Kirkegaard's distinction of aesthetical vs. ethical, the teacher's job is to break the spell of the aesthetic, that is, the immediate attraction of pleasure. One cannot learn while under the illusion that truth forms an objective system or while one practices the art of distance from reality by an aesthetic life. The teacher's chief task, then, is to break the spell of systematic thought and the absorption in aesthetic enjoyment. When one either does not look, or is content to enjoy pleasures, or when the pupil thinks truth is more complete than it ever can be, no learning can take place. The potential learner is under a spell which first must be broken, but naturally attempting to do this meets resistance. Teaching requires agility and maneuvering skill. There is no single formula to follow, since every individual case is different.

A fundamental change is necessary in the learner before teaching can be successful, and Kierkegaard states that only God can be the teacher in the situation of radical change. Of course, Augustine had said something like this before S.K., and everything depends on how much change is needed and who can be the author of this needed revolution. To teach, then, is not to convey information but to create the conditions for learning. Neither the student nor the teacher can be sure about maintaining control of this process. It follows no necessary dialectic, but at least we know what is needed. The chief function of the teacher is to make us aware, or to arouse our awareness.

As one reads what Kierkegaard says about Socrates as a teacher, S.K.'s interpretation makes Socrates sound more and more like Kierkegaard in Copenhagen than Socrates in Athens. Yet this makes it easy to see how, in his image of Socrates, S.K. himself viewed the role of the teacher. He comments frequently on Socrates' reported conflict with his wife, thus treating his role as a teacher of men as connected with female conflict, just as S.K. stresses his own unhappy love affairs. He also mentions Socrates' discontent with the established order, again suggesting that the teacher must somehow experience both personal and social alienation. Of course, S.K. paints Socrates chiefly as a teacher who demands that the student become a strong and independent self.

S.K. likes the traditional description of Socrates as the "gadfly" of Athens, but he portrays the prodding involved as playing on the individual's own passion, a phrase which perhaps describes S.K. more than Socrates. However, the basic aim, as S.K. reads Plato's dialogues, is to make the reader or hearer active. It is this which he sees as Socrates' basic teaching skill. The whole aim is to arouse the student's emotional response to draw out an independent decision. Socrates, S.K. says, feared most of all to be in error, so it is also the love of truth which drives the teacher in his art. At the base of it all, S.K. believes the problem is not so much to understand Socrates' teaching but to understand Socrates himself. He portrays Socrates as essentially unpopular, but this probably tells us more about S.K. as a teacher than Socrates.

Socrates, of course, always attracted a group when he spoke in the streets. It is S.K. who is the lonely figure and who writes in isolation as a silent communication. Socrates came into conflict with the authorities in Athens, but it is S.K. who seems to think this is a requirement for the serious teachers, although outwardly for most of his life he lived the existence of a successful and accepted citizen. S.K. paints Socrates in the image of the hero, but of course it is S.K. who is more obsessed with the notion of becoming a hero than Socrates. However, S.K.'s existentialism perhaps comes out most strongly in his contrast between Plato and Socrates.

Socrates, of course, left no written work or fixed doctrine, whereas Plato constructed a doctrine. S.K. himself writes, but it is still Socrates' non-dogmatic stance which intrigues him. He believes Plato gradually eliminated "the existential" (non-dogmatic, non-conclusive questioning) and substituted a system. Socrates, according to S.K., expressed the existential. He had no doctrine, no system. He had one only in his actions. Thus, Plato represents a misunderstanding of Socrates, in S.K.'s eyes, because he failed to grasp Socrates' notion of the teacher's role. Plato came to present his own doctrine; Socrates remained in the present moment. His teaching joined no historical stream that would allow the student to assimilate it into a fixed understanding. Rather, the teacher does not instruct, but by questioning constantly presses the student to his own decision, by his own action.

"Truth" is not the issue for the teacher. S.K. tells us he does not know if Christianity is true, but he will order his life *as if* it were and risk his life on that assumption. If it is not the truth, well then, all right. He will still have ventured for himself, which is the only way to learn. Socrates speaks "extemporaneously," S.K. thinks, and this expresses life more accurately than elaborately planned speeches. Of course, this is a romantic notion of the value of spontaneity. It overlooks the fact that Plato's dialogues, which almost alone preserve Socrates' memory, are not spontaneous speeches but elaborately and skillfully contrived pieces of art in writing. They do not record actual conversations in the raw but present Plato's point of view carefully articulated.

S.K. likes the image of Socrates as divinely commissioned to expose the ignorance of others, while not pretending to possess truth himself. He thinks that Socrates rejected the crowd and sought the "single individual," but of course the record seems to be that Socrates enjoyed crowds. Primitive inwardness, which S.K. wants to promote, means the elimination of historical knowledge; this leaves the person alone to face an idea. Not having lived in the 18th and 19th century Germany, Socrates could have had neither Hegel's trust in historical understanding nor S.K.'s violent reaction to it. As a teacher, Socrates is non-historical, but that is all it takes to please Kierkegaard. Socrates is one of a kind, an individual who stands out, and that is the way a teacher ought to live—for S.K.

Kierkegaard likes the Socratic (or Platonic) doctrine that truly to understand is to do or to be the knowledge. This notion that understanding is not understanding unless it is embodied in action (to know the good is to do the good) strikes a responsive cord with S.K. Of course, he is wise enough to realize that he likes Socrates at a distance as distilled through a literary gloss but might not have been able to endure him as a contemporary! S.K. does admit that he has an idealized view of Socrates and that he might have been more abrasive in person. However, Socrates' role is to break through aesthetic appreciation and to demand the ethical, the committed action. And that is the essential role of the teacher. Anyone can please a group by using passively accepted pleasant words, but the real function of the teacher is quite otherwise.

Socrates solved the problem of whether a teacher constructs a system and leaves it behind, because he did not write and took all of his wisdom with him to the grave. The teacher does not work for the accumulation of knowledge, as he is so often portrayed, but to encourage the student's ethical appropriation. Socrates best illustrated this by leaving behind no doctrine which his students could then simply follow. Socrates was only a personality. He did not have a system to impart, but to be an unforgettable personality and not a transmitter of beliefs is the primary teaching role. He alone is a teacher who himself expresses existentially what he teaches. S.K. thinks there are no teachers in his day, and he is called only to be an "assistant teacher." The only real deceivers are the so-called teachers who teach but whose lives do not express what they say in such appealing ways.

Necessity/Possibility

In one way, S.K.'s life as an author can be viewed as an attempt to escape from necessity into possibility. His polemic against Hegel and all abstract philosophy is aroused because he thinks both involve necessity and universality as their prime categories. He wants to stress possibility and the individual. The individual cannot be "the individual," which means to discover and develop one's true self, without the freedom which open possibilities allow. Necessity breeds conformity, and it is, for this reason, always a chief existential target. If the hold of necessity on the historical process can be broken, a future shaped by individual decision again becomes a possibility.

Of course, necessity is not "all bad." In *Authority and Revelation,* S.K. tells us necessity has the task of holding extreme views in check, because it demands a conformity to the original Christian revelation. In *The Attack Upon Christendom,* necessity is portrayed as something which had to be done. It is true that, later in life, S.K. came to realize more and more the abuses which sheer uncontrolled possibility leads to. As he saw freedom turn into license or even insanity, he recognized the need for some kind of holding point against absurdity. Of course, in spite of these later cautions, "subjectivity" is the main category S.K. feels needs most to be stressed. Necessity must be opposed because it makes it more difficult to recognize the subjective component which every decision requires.

In *The Concluding Unscientific Postscript,* S.K. asserts that "necessity must be dealt with by itself" (trans. David Swenson and Walter

Lowrie, Princeton University Press, 1944, p. 306). He concludes that importing necessity into the historical process has caused much confusion. The categories of possibility, of actuality, and of necessity have all been compromised. What S.K. is pleading for us to do is to restore some balance and to break the hold of any single category on our life and thought. Life must be lived in a balance, which makes it precarious and not subject to the unity reason hopes for. Wherever we have an uneasy balance of mutually exclusive categories, the security necessity brings with it is ruled out.

It is particularly interesting to note the connection between the categories of Necessity/Possibility in *The Concept of Dread* (trans. Walter Lowrie, Princeton University Press, 1946). We are not used to thinking of necessity and possibility in psychological terms, but it is characteristic of existentialism to restore psychology to a place of prominence. It uses depth experience as a tool in metaphysical construction. "Dread" swings the balance in our analysis of necessity, because "he who is educated by dread is educated by possibility" (p. 139). Abstractly considered, he might naturally side with necessity as the more important and comfortable concept, but abstract reasoning is not to be trusted just because it is detached. Where dread is experienced and taken seriously philosophically, possibility becomes fundamental and instructive.

S.K. remarks that possibility is "the heaviest of all categories" (p. 140) because of its link to the experience of dread. Necessity, by comparison, is "light" and easy, while dread is hard and difficult to bear. Ordinarily one hopes dread is a passing phenomenon and that when it comes it will not last. But possibility is linked to dread, and "he who is educated by possibility remains with dread" (p. 142). Our philosophical preference for necessity, of course, is inspired by the fact that possibility alone, without the action of a decisive will, induces the experience of dread. However, S.K. is convinced that anything else but the constant presence of dread is an escape from the realities of life.

This hard fact must be accepted if we are to achieve and to know freedom, since "dread is the dizziness of freedom . . . gazing down into its own possibility" (p. 55). To be free means to experience a dizziness, due both to the limitless abundance of the possibilities we perceive and because there is no effective determining control other than individual decisiveness. According to S.K.'s investigation of sin, dread comes into the world and human experience because no necessity drives men to sin. "If sin comes into the world by necessity . . . there is no dread" (p. 43). Dread and our constant awareness of its presence tells us of our own freedom, that is, if we listen to it. Psychological alertness and an inner sensitivity reveal what reality is like, whereas reason, if left to itself, might fool us into thinking of necessity as characteristic of life.

Of course, the classical source for S.K.'s discussion of necessity/possibility, and the occasion for the development of his own theories, lies in *Either/Or*. This is particularly true of the essay on "Equilibrium" (trans. David & Lillian Swenson, London: Oxford University Press, 1946, Vol. II), but S.K. also develops this theme in *Sickness Unto Death*. In S.K.'s contrast between the aesthetic and the ethical mode of life he most feels the need for decisiveness. He wants to stress the challenge which possibility presents in the formation of personality. The appeal to necessity is a dodge against decisiveness and leads to the error of not choosing in the right way (pp. 194–95). That is, when one is fooled and views himself only under the category of necessity, he avoids developing that decisiveness without which the self is really lost because it drifts.

Sickness Unto Death (trans. Walter Lowrie, New York: Doubleday and Co., 1954) takes up the theme of how the self is both formed and lost. It begins with the notion that "man is a synthesis of freedom and necessity" (p. 146). Man falls into sickness when he is paralyzed by the choices facing him. However, this situation is not to be despised, for it proves man's superiority over the beast to whom the vast realm of possibility is not open (p. 148). Human freedom, then, can never achieve a fixed condition, nor can necessity be ignored without dire risk. "Freedom is the dialectical element in the terms possibility and necessity" (p. 160). Thus, possibility is no good by itself since freedom can become lost in it. Necessity serves as a needed check against sheer wandering (p. 168).

Possibility, if it is left alone, has a tendency to go to destructive extremes. That is, it does so if the self dwells only on what is open to it as possibilities. Open possibility can become its own source of despair just as well as the bonds of necessity. "Now if possibility outruns necessity, the self runs away from itself, so that it has no necessity whereunto it is bound to return. . . . Then this is the despair of possibility" *(ibid.)*. But we learn a secret about reality through probing the source of the self's despair: "Actuality is a unity of possibility and necessity" (p. 169). Such a union is not produced automatically but depends on individual decision. He or she who cannot achieve this will not become a real person. He or she will remain abstracted and subject to control from outside.

We think of existentialism, at least at its extremes, as vaunting sheer possibility and the priority of the human will. But just as the subjective problem (human decisiveness) is always balanced by the objective problem (what is the case), so possibility must be controlled too. The soul can go astray in possibility, and it will do so whenever it lacks the power to obey itself or the norms set before it. That which is necessary in oneself does not arise to exert control automatically. It requires a firm decision on the individual's part in order to submit to what is necessary in oneself. The self is lost when one refuses to decide and allows necessary forces from within or without to control action. But the self can also be lost "owing to the fact that the self was seen fantastically reflected in the possible" (p. 170). A self which sees only open possibility before it is unreal. That is, it cannot face the demands of reality.

Amazingly enough, possibility provides the insight into God, and also the basis for a distinction between God and man. "The decisive thing is that for God all things are possible" (p. 171). This is the source of God's mystery too, since he combines necessity with this. Yet God is far more open to possibility than is man, who constantly fears for his own self destruction if he cannot control decision. "Personality is a synthesis of possibility and necessity" (p. 173). Thus, we know that God shares the central attribute of personality which it is man's goal to achieve. God holds in steady control what man holds in precarious balance. Here is their similarity and their difference. Thus, there is real reason for us to speak of man as made in God's image. Man uses God's control as a model for the self he wants to become.

The second classical source of S.K.'s thoughts on possibility/necessity come from the "interlude" in the *Philosophical Fragments* (trans. David Swenson and Howard Hong, Princeton University Press, 1962). As he discusses the quest for historical certainty, S.K. proposes a metaphysical revision of the central concepts under which we view reality. Necessity is thought to characterize the actual, but S.K. asks: "When the possible becomes actual, is it thereby made more necessary than it was?" (p. 89). His answer is no. It is false to view reality as necessary simply because it first springs from possibility. It does not, S.K. is convinced, become any more necessary in its process of transition into actuality.

Possibility is first linked with non-being, because it is not-yet. "But such a being which is nevertheless non-being, is precisely what possibility is" (p. 91). Thus, non-being now becomes primordial in reality. In fact necessity turns out to require a synthesis of possibility and actuality. "Nothing comes into existence with necessity" (p. 92). Whatever it controls, necessity does not govern the process by which living things are formed, although it may well fix the path of the stars.

"The actual is no more necessary than the possible, for the necessary is absolutely different from both" *(ibid.)*. All coming into existence takes place with freedom—this is Kierkegaard's basic thesis. "If the past is conceived as necessary, this can happen only by virtue of forgetting that it has come into existence" (p. 95). If necessity governed the historical process of coming into being, we would not be able to distinguish the past from the future, but in fact we do. Nevertheless, it is the future which arouses dread, not the past. This distinction convinces us of the need for both the future and possibility in our understanding of reality. These factors lead us to view history differently and link necessity more with reason than with life.

To know the past properly is *not* to know it as necessary. To know it correctly is to understand its base and source in possibility. Thus, knowledge of existence cannot be linked to necessity, and even knowledge once attained should be seen as rooted in possibility. In fact, we should marvel over the past. We see it aright when we feel the same sense of wonder about the past which we do about the outcome of the future. The uncertainty that is attached to possibility is the origin of our sense of wonder. This characterizes philosophy at its best too, not certainty. The past has the same quality of elusiveness that the future has, so that, properly understood, certainty can not be found in the past either.

Human doubt about existence cannot be overcome by historical study which hopes for the discovery of some necessity. Doubt, and its transformation to faith, require a free act of the will (p. 102). This affirms a man's position of decisiveness in spite of a lack of certainty. Belief and doubt are and should be more like passions than like knowledge (p. 103). When it is truly apprehended, the uncertainty present in the process of coming to be remains in the past and is never overcome. "At no time does the past become necessary" (p. 106). It remains as open as our future, except for the fact that its structure has already been decided by countless free acts. Belief and existence correspond to one another, and what exists in human life is not subject to a more secure mode of knowing.

As is true of all philosophers who follow the Platonic school, it is the self that becomes the model for understanding reality, not the other way around. The task of the self is freely to become itself, and this process in turn serves as our model for understanding the structure of reality. Just as necessity and possibility are equally needed in the process of becoming a self, since selves are made not born, we know that both aspects are equally primary in the constitution of reality. Neither possibility nor necessity can dominate reality or thought without distorting our understanding of both. Despair comes alike to the self with no necessity and to the self with no remaining open possibilities.

The self requires possibility just as much as necessity. Neither should dominate it, if our understanding is to be accurate or if the self is to become authentic. To understand such a self, the state of rest which reason habitually seeks cannot be applied. The task of the self and knowledge about it can never be complete. This lack of finality is not due to a failure on our part. Knowledge involving the self is not theoretically completeable, if we allow the insight of the experience of dread to form our view of reality. Like Plato's One and Many, possibility and necessity can neither be divorced from one another nor can either be allowed to dominate without introducing falsity into our understanding of existence. An uneasy tension and an incomplete dialectic remain with us and within reality. The rhythm of life is the swing from one pole to another, and the human task is to maintain our balance in the midst of this uncertainty.

Paradox/Passion

Almost anyone who knows anything about Søren Kierkegaard knows that he loved to stress the inevitability of paradox. Of course, he is by no means the first to do so. Hegel, whom he opposed bitterly, made paradox the life-spring of logic. But for Hegel and others, paradox challenges us and leads to difficulties, but it also leads to solutions. S.K.'s main point is that certain—but not all—paradoxes are ultimate and cannot be gone beyond. If Hegel says: thesis, antithesis, synthesis; S.K. says: thesis, antithesis, *no* synthesis. True, what is sometimes missed is that S.K. finds this impasse to be more true of subjective vs. objective problems. It is the involvement of the human individual who must decide for himself that so often renders paradox insoluble. Still, S.K. has come to oppose the rule that logic and reason are capable of resolving every human dilemma.

In the first place, we will be poorer if we eliminate all paradox, since paradox is the pathos of the intellectual life. Ordinary people may live simple lives, but great thinkers are exposed to paradoxes. The link which makes it possible to put all things together is missing, and this is a challenge to one who is alive in thought. Of course, S.K.'s prime illustration of paradox is Christianity with its doctrine of the incarnation, the assertion that God has become man, the eternal entered into the temporal. Christ's appearance is and was a paradox, and S.K.'s main opponent in this is the modern thought that we are in any better position today to explain the paradox than in earlier times. Science may have progressed, but man and Christianity are still the same.

It is, of course, easier for later generations to think they can remove the paradox. They do not see the visible Jesus, and so it is easier to represent him as the Son-of-God. For his own generation, Jesus was a paradox because he looked and talked like other human beings and yet was the Son-of-God. Now, however, the modern generation is shocked to find that he is human, that he spoke within the thought world of a particular age. Noticing this provincialism, they find a new paradox. How can someone who is part of his age in thought pattern really be the Son-of-God? That the Son-of-God became man, then, is and was the greatest metaphysical and religious paradox. Yet it would have been a greater paradox if the Son-of-God had become man, had walked around on earth, talked to us and still no one had detected who he was.

The divine paradox is that he became noticed. Otherwise God would have been the greatest ironist, to send his son but not to have him revealed. Even if God as man became noticed only by being crucified, still he was recognizable by his divine authority, S.K. tells us, even though faith is demanded to solve the paradox. Our foolish human understanding might have preferred that Jesus influenced his age and advanced it, but his divinity only led to crucifixion. For this reason all Christianity is rooted in paradox. In that sense, Christianity ought not to want to be understood. Christianity entered the world not to be understood but to exist in it and to provoke response. If we rationalize it away, we rob it of its power to challenge us.

Of course, S.K. is always clear to point out that the paradox only arises by the joining of eternal truth with an existing individual. This point is similar to Camus' notion of the "absurd." The world is not absurd in itself. It becomes so only when placed in relationship to the human demand for pure rationality we put upon it. What we demand by way of value and meaning and purpose becomes absurd in relation to the quiet, unresponsive, factual world. In itself the world simply is. It only appears absurd in relation to man's demands. So it is the bringing together of God and man, divine demands and human frailty, that produces the paradox. God alone and man alone are not paradoxical, but their union is.

Furthermore, in Christianity God chose to reveal himself in suffering, and the notion that the eternal can suffer does produce paradox.

The problem is that human understanding will not admit that there is something it cannot understand. Kierkegaard comes at the end of a long age of science and rationalism, and he faces a human scholarship and science that is arrogant about the limitless powers of its ability to understand. When this happens, S.K. thinks it spreads confusion, because the task of human knowing is to understand that there is something it cannot understand, and then to understand what that is and why. Moreover, if human understanding will take the trouble to try to understand itself, S.K. is convinced it will not find pure rationalism but the very source of unavoidable paradox. (Here, of course, he is opposed to Freud and in agreement with Jung.)

In modern dress, all Kierkegaard is doing is returning to medieval or traditional mysticism at the end of an age of rationalism, one thesis of which is that nothing is beyond the grasp of human understanding if properly analyzed. Another but forgotten interpretation is that the power of human understanding is to recognize what it cannot understand and to be able to give an account of why. Human understanding is not helpless. It is able to recognize its own limits. However, only those who are willing to struggle can see this, not the many who do not work hard enough to discover their limits. Thus, paradox cannot become popular, because only those who finally struggle to a certain vantage point of inner vision can see its source.

A popular answer comes quickly and takes the form of a yes or a no. S.K. says this is the outlook of a college student. But if the answer takes ten years and comes in the form of a system, such that it is not quite clear whether he knows it or not, this is a speculative answer, and that person is either a philosophy professor or he ought to be one. S.K.'s main targets are the pretensions of human reason which admit no limitations and proceed as if nothing were beyond its grasp. Kierkegaard thinks God is more obscure after his revelation in Jesus than before. The revealed God is more incomprehensible than the unrevealed God. Why? Because he is revealed as a God of love and yet the world is full of evil. Evil and senseless destruction are not paradoxical in themselves. But when a God of love is introduced, they become insoluble contradictions.

S.K. remarks that he is mixed up by having been brought up as a Christian. Why? Because his youthful Sunday school made God seem easy and obvious, whereas the truth is that it is still impossible to identify God directly. S.K. sets up the law of remoteness: The more God is presented as present, to the same degree God is distanced. When Christianity was not a doctrine but was simply expressed in one's life, God was closer to actuality then than when Christianity became a doctrine. When there were no clergy but all Christians were brothers, God was closer to actuality than when there came to be many clergymen and a powerful ecclesiastical order. Then came churches, so many great and splendid churches, and God was distanced to the same degree. The history of Christianity is the progressive removal of God by tactfully and politely building churches, doctrinal systems, and monuments with men inside who speak easy words.

It is with the single individual (who is S.K.'s favorite) that the solution lies. Every individual is able to venture, and S.K. is sure God is willing to become involved with the one who is willing to venture. There are preachers and professors who want to make a profit, but where is there one who will actually venture, he asks? Church councils are called and presumably when they convene God is present. But S.K. is convinced God relates inversely to mass displays and is most present to the one, solitary, destitute, abandoned human being. This is the place for God. This is the paradox of Christianity, and when it is removed we have simply returned to paganism.

Of course, S.K. stresses paradox because he is convinced his age is without passion. It has grown cold and dull. Yet he does not intend to sanction every rare passion. S.K.'s definition of the origin of passion is rather carefully developed. The age needs pathos, because its tragedy is to be an age only of reason and reflection. So the question is how to break this stultifying grip? There are many people able to live without any real consciousness penetrating their lives. In this way they live on in unclarity. They are resigned to life, but they never distinguish between resignation and faith based on passion. Since passion is the source of faith for S.K., a rationalistic age, one which removes or stifles passion, cannot know genuine religious faith. If faith has disappeared, we should ask why and whether it is our own doing.

Although he stresses subjectivity, S.K. can admit that Christianity has an objective existence too. What does not exist here, however, is the kind of passion which is the formal condition of being able to receive the content of Christianity. If we complain of a lack of faith, it is our own fault for removing or ridiculing passion and thinking that faith could somehow still support itself. Of course, if we think reason can comprehend and provide us with everything we need to know, or more importantly, all we need for our survival as existing human beings, then we eliminate passion as if it were an improvement to be without it. However, if paradox in at least one case is not removable, passion returns and so does human vitality.

Possibility/Actuality

Like most existentialists, S.K. claims that he is opposed to speculative metaphysics. Nevertheless, it is primarily the abstract metaphysics of Hegel which he objects to so violently. This nowhere becomes more evident than in S.K.'s use of "possibility/actuality," since he really forms a new metaphysics with this pair of concepts. The fundamental novelty he develops becomes one of the cornerstones of his work and a key to his understanding.

Of course, as is characteristic, S.K.'s approach is at first psychological. It is both his penetration of mood and his new insight into the self which allow him to see possibility in a new relation to actuality. This offers us an approach to philosophy with a new perspective. In *The Concept of Dread* (trans. Walter Lowrie, Princeton University Press, 1946), possibility is presented as the intoxicant which psychology and ethics use to dodge the consequences of sin. They consider only sin's possibility, while the need is to explore sin's real origins (p. 21).

In a state of innocence, the synthesis needed to constitute man is not yet actual. He lives as yet only in possibility (p. 44). It means, "I can." But possibility does not easily pass over into actuality, except in abstract thought. "Dread" is introduced as the driving force necessary to commit man. It moves possibility from the play of thought into actuality. Dread does this by forcing a leap. Thus actuality comes about, not by a smooth transition, but suddenly and freely. There is no necessity determining the passage. Dread arises just because we see that necessity does not lead us from possibility to actuality. This transition comes about only by the determination of freedom.

Possibility is an abyss (p. 55) which, when it is experienced psychologically, produces dread and the dizziness of freedom that in turn leads to sin and to man's fall. If possibility moved easily to actuality, this would not be the case. When freedom gazes into its own possibility, then each spirit seeks a synthesis which can give it stability. Instead of accomplishing this, it often is overcome and falls into chaos, experiencing dread in its attempt to bring some possibility out of necessity. In dread there is an egoistic infinity of possibility, which is not a definite choice but rather a cause for alarm. The fact that some actions are sinful is hidden from the innocent one, but this knowledge itself opens new possibilities when it is uncovered. Yet the self, when it sees the freedom of possibility latent in the sensuous, falls into even greater dread (p. 66).

However, S.K.'s novel explorations into the psychological effect of possibility and freedom lead him to stress the future as more important for our understanding than history. "The possible corresponds precisely to the future" (p. 82). For freedom, the possible is the future, but the individual experiences a dread which neither the actual nor the historical alone could induce. We move away from actuality when we turn to the past, since the problem of actuality lies only in the future and in man's freedom in relation to possibility. Our dread never arises over what is fixed, so the presence of dread forces us toward the future. We move to confront possibility, and this moves us away from any simple interest in the past. Our main task always lies ahead.

Because it is freedom and the future which must be released, possibility is our only educator and dread is the mood induced (p. 139). Dread is the possibility of freedom, and it is not discoverable in actuality. Dread educates us by opening up possibility, and we must learn to deal with infinity. This makes possibility not easy but rather a heavy burden to bear (p. 140). Luck and good fortune are also possibilities, but possibility includes the dreadful as well as the fortunate, since everything is possible. The individual learns to discover the possibility in himself and to shape that from which he is to learn. But surely this is no easy or obvious task which is as ready-made for us as history is. Actuality is not as critical a test for the self as possibility is.

On the other hand, actuality also educates when it is taken as reality. This makes it the opposite of a melancholy tendency to hide in possibility and a refusal to face life as it is. (*Stages on Life's Way,* trans. Walter Lowrie, New York: Shocken Books, 1967). The religious life is contrasted to mere possibility, because it demands more commitment (p. 242). When "inflection-possibilities" (p. 253) are continually tossed out for consideration, this obscures decision because it keeps one constantly engrossed in thought. Possibilities intoxicate. Melancholy is a condensation of possibility (p. 385), so that we see one source of melancholy as the inability to move out of possibility into an actuality which is freely selected. Simply considering all possibilities becomes a hiding place that keeps one from realizing what actuality requires from us for decisive existence.

S.K., of course, almost defines faith as "possibility." What is humanly impossible (e.g., both Isaac's death at Abraham's hand *and* that Abraham should also keep his son) becomes possible for God. And here it is the poetic tendency which keeps one back from actuality and involvement, an impasse which is broken only by an act. That is, the poetic is dispelled for S.K. by challenging the *Corsair,* and the ethical is challenged for Abraham by obeying the direction to sacrifice Isaac.

A poet is one who has his life and his actuality in different categories from that of his literary production. Thus, we can see S.K.'s later life is an attempt to move both his authorship and his life onto the same plane of mutuality. Ethical communication will use the medium of actuality. *Armed Neutrality* (trans. Howard and Edna Hong, New York: Simon & Schuster, 1968) represents such a shift for S.K., from indirect communication and a poetic approach to action in a situation of actuality. And Christianity needs to be placed in a context of actuality, i.e., outside of churches. S.K. constantly struggles with himself as to whether he, as an author, is the man to do this. That is, he does so until "the change" and his time of *Attack.* "Actuality" comes to have many of the connotations we associate with existentialism, because it involves thought and decisions that are made in, and are forced by, the seriousness of life. vs. the aesthetic man whose life remains detached in possibility.

On the stage of historical actuality, the martyr learns what Christianity is by suffering for it—and this must be suffering in more than thought. Christianity has the element of the absolute, which is all right as long as it is held in thought and in ideal only. But any attempted action in life will bring it into collision with actuality (p. 102). *Fear and Trembling* results because the man who pursues religion comes into conflict with reality due to God's demands. Without such a clash forced upon him, he would live in repose in religious ideals. Yet if such confrontation with reality brings the day of testing upon the religious man, it is possibility which is largely responsible for the *Sickness Unto Death* (trans. Walter Lowrie, New York: Doubleday & Co., 1954). Since the self is a synthesis, man risks the possibility of falling into despair at every moment if the synthesis cannot be sustained or achieved.

To be a spirit means to be open to infinite possibility, but to achieve a stable self means to compose a synthesis between the finite and infinite. Freedom is not sheer possibility but rather "the dialectical element in the terms possibility and necessity" (p. 168). Despair comes from the failure of freedom, that is, the failure to relate to God. If God is ignored, we cannot hold possibility in check by necessity, since only the divine life represents that capacity. The self can become fantastic, if it loses itself in the possible, cavorting wildly with no internal restraint. Possibility and necessity are equally required for stability (p. 168). Necessity serves as a check and keeps the self from running away from itself. The "despair of possibility" sets in when possibility outruns necessity and has no check (p. 169).

Yet nothing becomes actual when more and more becomes possible, and the reality of the self is to be found in actuality, or in the unity of possibility and necessity. The abyss of possibility swallows up the self in infinity when it is unchecked. If this happens, it is necessity which a man lacks. Then the soul goes astray in possibility and falls into despair. He has lost the power to obey what is necessary and no limit can be set on the self. The self is lost when it is seen fantastically reflected in the possible (p. 170) and when no necessity forces it to relate to actuality. For God, all things are possible, but this is not true for men who force themselves to become actual selves, that is, who accept individual responsibility. Without possibility a man cannot breathe, but a man can also lose himself in possibility by losing the power to obey. "Personality is a synthesis of possibility and necessity" (p. 173).

When this cooperation fails, one falls into despair, or despair is revealed as having been present. But when this happens, at least he is a step closer to realizing what the task before him is. Sin for S.K. lies in the will, not the intellect (p. 226). It is the will's problem either to empower the effort for synthesis or else to allow the spirit to run away from the task by hiding its despair in a quest for immediate happiness. "Faith" in part comes to mean the willingness to accept the burden of achieving the required synthesis of the self.

S.K. normally shuns dialectical metaphysical construction, but in the "Interlude" in the *Philosophical Fragments* he achieves his clearest statement on possibility/actuality (trans. David Swenson and Howard Hong, Princeton University Press, 1962). What is possible is made actual freely and by an act of the will, but S.K. wants to exclude necessity from characterizing this process (p. 89). All that comes into existence is changed by suffering in transition, so that nothing that is possible comes to exist as it was first conceived but only as it has been altered by the process. Possibility is a being "which is nevertheless non-being" (p. 91).

Thus, possibility is akin to non-being and is the opposite of actuality. What is necessary cannot change or suffer, so that the possibility which becomes actual shows by its passing through this process that the procedure is not necessary but free. Necessity becomes a synthesis of possibility and actuality. But nothing comes into existence with necessity alone. "The actual is no more necessary than the possible, for the necessary is absolutely different from both" (p. 92). All coming into being takes place with freedom. When we think of the past as necessary, we do so only by forgetting the free process by which it first came into being (p. 95). The historical is now a fact, but it is not thereby necessary.

Future and past stand on the same ground. Neither is more necessary than the other and both are made out of possibility, either as selected as or yet to be selected. To assume to predict the future and to pretend to understand the past are really the same thing (p. 95). Neither one is necessary, although we may be fooled by the actuality which the past now has achieved. If we do this, it is only accomplished by an act of forgetting how what is possible first comes to be. Simply having knowledge of the past confers no necessity upon it (p. 99). Since it is rooted in possibility, understanding the past is like prophecy in relation to the future. The historian should confront the past "moved by the emotion which is the passionate sense for coming into existence: wonder" (p. 99).

The historical, for S.K., has the elusiveness implicit in all coming into existence. This illustrates the fundamental role which possibility plays in his metaphysics and the sense of freedom which characterizes the whole structure of being, including actuality. "Doubt can be overcome only by a free act, an act of will" (p. 102), and this makes faith a required condition-decision and not a form of knowledge. Belief and doubt are opposite passions (p. 105), and no natural equilibrium can be achieved without employing belief. The structure we face is rooted too much in uncertainty (possibility) to yield knowledge on its own without first adding the passion of belief.

Belief and coming into existence correspond to one another, so that the uncertainty implicit in all coming into existence will continue for the one seeking to know the event, if he sees it clearly. This happens for the historian just as it did for the contemporary involved in the original decision process of choosing between possibles (p. 106). "It is an illusion to suppose that it is easier to understand after an event than before" (p. 107). The uncertainty we associate with determining the future exists for the past, too, if we see it properly—that is, as rooted in possibility and not necessity. Aristotle wanted to use necessity as a baseline from which to understand contingency. S.K. proposes to reverse that fundamental role and to see possibility as pervasive. If so, necessity becomes only an achievement of decision and will, and it can never be more stable than that.

S.K. wants to make the accidental just as necessary as the necessary (*Either/Or*, trans. David and Lillian Swenson, London: Oxford University Press, 1946, p. I–191). The young always have an eye for the potential, and thus they see the possible with a passionate sense (p. I–33). Yet, possibilities have a way of changing into impossibilities as the years pass by, which represents the problem of decision.

One of S.K.'s most penetrating analyses of the problem of constituting the self out of possibility and freedom is presented in his essay on "Equilibrium." The aesthetic life stresses possibility alone in its attempt to seek refuge from consistency and responsibility. The ethical life, on the other hand, requires strict adherence. The trick of life is to keep an equilibrium between these two unresolvable components. There is an "instant of choice" (p. 138) when it is indifferent what a man chooses. However, if he lets that decisive moment slip by, it may not return. Or, it can be opened again as an option only with great difficulty. The choice is decisive for the content of personality, since no self is given a single set of possibles to start with but floats on a sea which essentially is unlimited.

Thus, no possible can become real for the personality without the decisive power of choice being added. Actuality is not a natural end-result for all possibility. Rather it comes about only by the intervention of personality. Or, we might say, personality is shaped in the midst of the action necessary to bring some possibilities to actuality and to exclude others—if we accept responsibility for the choice. The choice among possibles can be made unconsciously or by obscure powers within the self, but if it is the latter actuality becomes fate and not freedom. If the personality is aware of the danger involved, it will seize the instant in which the course of the future is indifferent, and it moves to change that course in the decisive moment.

It is a sensitivity to these crucial moments which defines the personality and opens the future to freedom. This is not caprice but a synthesis of possibility and necessity achieved in that fleeting open moment. "It is important to choose and to choose in time" (p. 139). If one shifts constantly from one possibility to another and is never able to hold to a choice between two alternatives in the moment, that personality drifts on. Some choices, of course, are not decisive enough to achieve actuality because they are not made seriously but only aesthetically. That is, they are made so that they may be changed at any instant and undone. Possibility itself is not sufficient to sustain actuality. It requires an ethical decisiveness on the part of the personality if the resulting actuality is to have any staying power.

Neutrality is the vice of actuality, since it takes a committed and decisive choice to sustain actuality. Possibility can open the door to freedom, but it does not have enough power on its own to sustain itself against the choices which must be made. Since actuality has such a plastic nature, it may be molded either hard or soft from possibility. However, the necessity needed to hold the mold in the chosen form is supplied by the later decisiveness of a personality, one which remains continually open to act in the crucial moment.

Of course, to one who views life aesthetically, possibility is much more attractive than actuality, and we all attempt to avoid decisiveness. The modern method of proclaiming Christianity, S.K. tells us, is to suppress the impossible aspects and to stress the probable aspects. This obscures God, for S.K. is sure that possibility is offered as a hint from God which a person must follow. If you trust in God you will venture on the possible and feel content to have tried even if you fail. Not to venture is to be unhappy and in torment. The problem is that the attractions of the aesthetical life caution one against venturing for fear of disturbing the pleasantries of life. Kierkegaard sees God as essentially risk taking.

We have limited God by the narrowness of our imagination. Our imagination does not stretch far enough to think of all the possibilities open to us, and for some reason we extend this to say that God does not have possibilities open to him. God has 100,000 possibilities open at every moment without any one of them being a miracle, but our human arbitrariness wants to cut this off for God, because we no longer see any possibilities. There is a great deal of difference if we understand something as possible rather than as actual. Possibility is easy to admit, but actuality is more difficult to assess. Christianity's intention is that one must use his life to venture, so we should not avoid affirmation. We make possibilities into poetry and relate to them in imagination. Christianity presents a God who ventures into actuality and expects man to learn how to move out of comfortable possibilities into the risk of becoming actual.

Repetition/Freedom

"Repetition," insofar as it refers to S.K.'s little book by that title, is not the subject of our concern. The question of the background for that book and its place in S.K.'s writings as a whole is one thing. The meaning of the concept of "repetition" in S.K.'s thought in general, however, is an equally important matter. As would be expected with an author like Kierkegaard, the fact that this idea finally became a single book is important for our understanding of his authorship in general. In what sense, we need to ask, can S.K.'s whole work be understood under the concept of "repetition"? In addition to issuing in one book, how did that idea insinuate itself in the whole work and life of our author?

In the first place, S.K. is much attracted to the figure of Socrates. He represents in his person, as he has for so many, what philosophy is. The *Philosophical Fragments* is S.K.'s best statement on the function of philosophy and of his own use of Socratic thought, but it also represents an important change away from Socrates. Platonic recollection and dialectic stand in contrast to the central place S.K. gives to repetition. On the practical side, S.K. stresses repetition to contrast himself with Hegel and his followers and their use of dialectic. However, it is Socrates—and S.K.'s own advance beyond him—that holds the key to his ability to launch a new philosophical starting point.

We know that some of S.K.'s contemporaries at first could see no serious meaning in his book on repetition. Therefore, we have to ask how his exploration of a humorous notion led him to a more serious philosophical discovery. If S.K.'s contemporaries misunderstood the importance he gave to repetition, "misunderstanding" might be crucial and also connected with the notion of repetition, too. Repetition seems like a trivial and a light notion at first. Yet, like Kierkegaard's love of the accidental because it is more instructive than the necessary, the humorous idea of repetition may also contain informative value.

We are forced into repetition only if originally we are misunderstood. Or, we may be misunderstood because we engage in repetition in order to create misunderstanding. We know that S.K. was misunderstood at times and that he considered these experiences a necessary preliminary to being able to state the truth. Thus, "repetition" assumes an important place as a philosophical condition for understanding. S.K. did repeat himself often: in his experiences, by his revisit to Berlin; in the themes he uses; and by developing the same notion in *Fear and Trembling* and then again in *Sickness Unto Death*. However, the problem is to grasp how the repetition present in his writings, e.g., the old themes he continually returns to, is a key to understanding what is instructive about them.

In the first place, the function of both the "moment" and the "temporal" are involved in all this. S.K.'s difference from Socrates stems from the fact that understanding in recollection is neither a temporal condition nor is it dependent on either the moment or the occasion of its grasp. Repetition, then, is important just because it concentrates attention on the moment. It makes us aware of the temporal, and it is also needed in order to cut the cord of an otherwise relentlessly advancing dialectic. His "Project of Thought" as stated in *Philosophical Fragments* is: "How far does truth admit of being learned" (chapter 1). The effect of repetition on S.K. is to call both Platonic recollection and Hegelian dialectic into doubt. He is convinced that neither has advanced the question beyond its original starting point.

The appearance of repetition reveals the extreme situation of the seeker after truth, as S.K. outlines this in the *Fragments.* The basic adequacy of the knower is challenged if knowledge does not advance but merely returns to an earlier position where it remains fixed. Repetition shows us the need for a teacher who is more than an accidental occasion, if the learner is to do more than merely grasp what is eternal and is already possessed internally. Repetition reminds us of the human quality in all knowledge and the frail condition of the knower. It reveals our essential dependence and our lack of ability to advance by individual or group effort. This induces the humility necessary if any future change is to be decisive. Repetition appears not to be an advance. Yet, without its chastening effect, no real advance is possible.

Kierkegaard also connects "freedom" to the concept of repetition, and this again argues for its centrality in his thought. The aesthetic man craves novelty in order to sustain his non-serious way of life. Thus, he fears repetition as being both boring and confining, but life makes it impossible for anyone to avoid repetition for very long. When repetition catches him, the aesthetic man, if he craves his personal freedom, should follow the advice given in "The Rotation Method" (*Either/Or,* Vol. 1). He must learn the shrewdness that accepts repetition as the challenge to achieve an inventiveness that makes into a novel occasion what otherwise would be a repetition of the same experience. To do this demands a clever subjective appropriation by an aesthetic master.

Yet "repetition" raises two subtle philosophical problems which when properly understood it also helps to solve: (1) How can psychology play a role in our appropriation of fundamental philosophical principles?; and (2) Metaphysically speaking, how can what has existed in the past receive new being in the present? Thus repetition becomes a new way of raising the problem of "time." It is "solved" to the extent that repetition helps us understand why we need not be the merciless victims of time but can learn to arrest its relentless march. Psychology enters into our consideration because the aesthetic mood must be broken before time can be either understood or transcended.

S.K. is a "repetitious" writer. That is, the same themes reappear in many of his works at many stages, e.g., the broken engagement, the poetic vs. the religious spirit. To understand S.K.'s work as an author you need to do more than just understand his essentially religious purpose, as he will tell us about it in the *Point of View.* The reader needs to understand why he repeats and comes back to a small set of basic themes so many times, e.g., marriage, dread. What possible edification can result from such repetition? How and why can this move the psyche to deeper insights? In *Stages on Life's Way* S.K. even repeats the theme of repetition, but now he wants to move it further, away from the aesthetic. Without repetition perhaps no advance is possible, since life is controlled by no automatic dialectic. If nothing moves us forward necessarily, repetition may, strangely enough, contain the power we need to advance.

In the *Point of View* S.K. prefers the notion of "dialectical reduplication" as his theme. Yet the *Point of View* is in some sense also a repetition. In it S.K. reviews and repeats once again all or most of the themes he has already dealt with. By repeating and reviewing he has deepened his insight further. He also makes his reader repeat the same thought movements over again, although this time they are altered, which is what happens with repetition. In rehearsing his authorship in *Point of View*, S.K. is stung to discover certain similarities between himself and Adler's work, and he discussed this in *Authority and Revelation*. He published his own *Repetition* pseudonymously with two other books in one year, but he does not find Adler's rapid literary production equally stimulating. Evidently repetition is a subtle art—if one is to accept it in one case and reject it in another.

The problem is to transform repetition into something inward, and it is the failure to do this that plunges any spirit into despair. Repetition can be an aesthetic art form, but it can also be a religious way of life. Eternity is the true repetition our present day religious life tries to imitate. Eternity lies ahead, not behind as it did for the Greeks, and repetition is the category by which one enters eternity forward. Repetition can however become a mere habit, whenever the eternal goes out of it. The religious life, when it is rightly understood, seeks to prevent that loss. "When originality is lacking in repetition we have habit" *The Concept of Dread,* (trans. Walter Lowrie, Princeton University Press, 1957, p. 132). Only seriousness can prevent this, and repetition brings with it the seriousness of existence.

Sickness Unto Death (trans. Walter Lowrie, Princeton University Press, 1954) is called a "repetition" (p. 134) of *Fear and Trembling,* one of S.K.'s earliest works. As such it furnishes a good example of how repetition characterizes S.K.'s work as an author. *Fear and Trembling* dealt with the question of faith, whereas *Sickness Unto Death* deals with the question of the self, of sin, and of healing. In no strict sense, then, is the one a repetition of the other. Nevertheless, S.K. takes certain themes in Christian experience and in his life, and he returns to them time and again. His aesthetic themes, of course, are developed differently. But where religion is concerned, insight comes through the deepening acquired by constantly returning to a theme, a liturgical repetition.

Among his aesthetic writings, "The Rotation Method" in the first volume of *Either/Or* (trans. David and Lillian Swenson, revised Howard A. Johnson, Princeton University Press, 1971) provides an excellent contrast. The rotation method is perhaps the prime example of an aesthetic technique. One does repeat small items so as not to tire of the constant race for novelty, but this should be done so that subtle changes make the repeated act seem fresh. This keeps life on the surface and prevents either attaching the individual to the event or allowing it to penetrate into his nature. The repetition of religious themes involved in *Sickness,* on the other hand, is specifically meant to alter the self by deepening reflection on a familiar theme.

Boredom is the malaise the rotation method seeks to escape. The sickness of sin, on the other hand, is something that requires a deepened penetration into the structure of the self. Only a fundamental altering can cure this fault. Repetition, of course, is involved in the ethical life, as it is presented in the second volume of *Either/Or.* To marry is to will the repetition necessary to transform immediate love into something more lasting, something that holds the self back from constant and destructive change. The self needs to achieve an equilibrium between its aesthetic and its ethical component, and repetition is important in accomplishing this. The aesthetical alone moves you along constantly and prevents choice by its rush to enjoy. The definitive choice, so necessary for the ethical life, requires the element of willed repetition to sustain it.

The aesthetic life seeks to immerse itself in a mood, but the intrusion of repetition will break any mood and reintroduce the question of ethical commitment. The aesthetic life is interested in beauty and seeks change. The ethical, however, can reveal its own beauty, but this comes through willed repetition and the constancy that makes life beautiful by its stability. Repetition gives to the ethical life this beauty through consistency, because it develops the equilibrium in the self without which the self would fall into despair. Thus, the anxiety of dread, which of all moods does the most to destroy happiness, is countered by consciously admitting repetition. The result is the maturity of life.

In *The Concluding Unscientific Postscript* (trans. David Swenson & Walter Lowrie, Princeton University Press, 1944) S.K. develops his famous definition of "subjective truth." He also deepens his notion of the religious life, and he begins to reflect on his work to date. What his age lacks, he asserts, is inwardness. His contemporaries had forgotten how to exist, S.K. thought, and repetition is a useful tool to remedy this dilemma. It forces inwardness and prevents a person from living a life totally absorbed in outward mood. *Repetition* had been called a psychological experiment. S.K.'s comments about this in the *Postscript* tell us something about both repetition and his role as an author. Any "experiment" will create a chasm between reader and author. A separation of inwardness is generated between them. Now the relationship reaches a crucial, and perhaps enlightening, stage.

Thus, all authorship should aim at creating inwardness and repetition, just as a psychological experiment does this. It will isolate the reader so that he must arrive at his own decision in inwardness—or at least that is the hope. The aim is to move the author and reader "away from one another in inwardness" (p. 236), and repetition is indispensable for achieving this. If any literary production is to be significant, "it should always have passion" *(ibid.)*, and repetition is a passion-builder. The individual who has undergone any trial returns to existence in the ethical, and this is the aim of all good writing. The author should challenge the reader by leaving him in the lurch and by not offering the conclusion the reader wants in order to bolster his security.

If it is the absence of an ending which is necessary to produce the inwardness of the religious disposition. Since it returns again and does not move, repetition is an ideal instrument. "The absence of a result is precisely the determination of inwardness" (p. 257). S.K. himself returns to his earlier works and examines their themes again. In that sense his authorship is a "repetition," that is, a constant renewal of earlier themes. Yet, it is clear both in the *Postscript* and *Point of View* that his repetition of earlier themes actually advances his insight.

There is a change in his authorship, one that is largely brought about by his returning to repeat earlier themes but in different ways. He understands the original questions differently by repeating them and by the inwardness which this reflection causes.

For example, in the *Philosophical Fragments,* S.K. repeats his favorite theme of Socratic understanding, or of the frequent misunderstanding of Socrates' mission. In the course of this analysis, he moves "beyond Socrates." He develops his own view that there is a radical error in the learner's situation and that the learner lacks the possession of even the condition for knowledge. This is opposed to Socrates' theory of recollection. Where authorship is concerned, S.K. likes to use a dialogue form of involvement with his reader. But does he deepen his notion of indirect communication, a technique much used by Socrates, by his own continued return to the theme? Repetition points the way back, and then on, to an increased inner reflection.

His book on *Repetition* itself (trans. Walter Lowrie, Harper & Row, 1964) provides an illustration of this phenomenon. S.K.'s contemporaries could detect no serious purpose in this work. Thus, when he felt the reviews did not do it justice, he returned to his book and its defense by writing a new preface. His repetition of the original theme deepens the concept amazingly. His novel idea becomes clear only in this repetition of *Repetition.* The distance created by the misunderstanding of his readers forces S.K. back into himself to search for a deeper understanding. Freedom, when it is defined as pleasure fears repetition (p. 11) he says. However, no inventiveness can keep repetition away forever and so pleasure falls into despair. This observation induces the discovery of "the rotation method," yet this shrewdness will ultimately despair too, and then repetition is introduced.

Freedom becomes repetition, and it fears only change away from what has become so instructive. Yet beyond all this stands the religious movement as the true expression of repetition. Repetition and the struggle to avoid it brought S.K. (and will bring others) to this stage in life. The young, of course, see repetition as only an outward problem, just as S.K. did in his revisit to Berlin and the attempt to recapture his youth. But repetition must be found within the individual. "Step by step he discovers repetition, being educated by existence" (p. 14). When you try to make repetition into an outward form and search for it in geography or history, the despair of possibility is created. However, this can lead us to inwardness and to discover the locus of the true possibility of repetition.

In giving his explanation of *Repetition,* S.K. deepens and expands the concept without simply repeating it. Yet he begs the pardon of the book for violating its individuality in making obvious what it preferred to hide (p. 13). So it is with S.K. as an author. Much is hidden in the writing which does not make its intention clear, and one is forced by repetition (unless he turns away from S.K. in disgust) to repeat again and again in an attempt to understand. "Once through lightly" simply will not do where Søren Kirkegaard is concerned. His mass of writing is too heterodox and too indirect to permit direct grasp. Thus, S.K.'s stress on the need to use indirect communication is connected to the idea of repetition. What we put in indirect form can seldom be understood if it is passed by quickly. Indirect communication requires repetition to disclose its meaning.

This becomes clear when one compares S.K.'s later accounts of *Repetition* with the theme of the book itself, which actually is highly whimsical. Yet, when he is forced to return to the themes, S.K. himself becomes more serious and gives us one of his more profound statements on metaphysics. The problem is to transform repetition into something inward and to set freedom's task as that of realizing repetition. S.K. was "misunderstood" by Heiberg who reviewed the book, but this taught S.K. the virtues of being misunderstood, both for himself and for his readers. To be forced to repeat what the author did not make clear the first time may lead to new inner understanding which is not obtainable in any easier way.

We need to contrast "repetition" with Greek "recollection," although repetition is recollected forwards and not repeated backwards. One recalls what is behind him, which involves a certain area of unhappiness (pp. 33–34), but if he is able to master repetition one also learns courage. The beauty of life is here, but it can be missed by the one who does not have the courage to move back constantly—and also forward and toward novelty.

"Repetition is reality, and it is the seriousness of life" (p. 35). And S.K. suggests that this quality is also fundamental to God's life.

The willing of repetition is required if anything is to be brought into existence by God or man. God had the courage to will the repetition of his relationship to this creation, rather than to move forward constantly to some new creation which might be more exciting for God. The world as constituted is boring, but God wills it in repetition and deepens his own religious attitude. Interestingly enough, it is in this context that S.K. raises the question of the "deceitful author" (p. 35). That is, he is one who uses deceit not to mislead but in order to force his reader to grasp what he has said with the same energy the author first had to use to carry thought to such extremes. Communication requires equal and opposite energy on the part of the reader to grasp what a serious author purposely hides in inwardness rather than trying to expose it directly. Where thought is not made direct in order to protect the reader's freedom of decision, repetition is also made necessary. Otherwise the serious conclusion might be passed by.

S.K.'s subject in *Repetition* is a young boy in love. This youth can already recollect his love, and so he is essentially through it before it has begun. He stands at the end of life instead of at its beginning. Thus, if he is not to fall into despair, he needs the vitality to take this "death" and transform it back into life. He must will the repetition of the first moment. Failure to do this will awaken his poetic spirit, so that this gives us some insight into the origin of S.K.'s poetic gifts too. He was through his love affair almost before it began, and he could not will to start it over again, that is, to will repetition. This drove him to despair, to inwardness, to poetic expression in authorship, although finally to a public outburst of protest, too.

To understand repetition is to overcome the unhappiness of recollection. You will an earlier life to be new again, but not simply as a past which one can touch only in thought. The soul must gain "the elasticity of irony" (p. 48). The love of recollection is unhappy, but, "if the young man had believed in repetition" (p. 49), what inwardness he might have attained! "When one does not possess the categories of recollection or of repetition the whole of life is resolved into a void and empty noise" (p. 53). Repetition is the interest of metaphysics, too, since it is the only action capable of inducing reflection of a type that reaches the serious depths of life. In order to grasp basic structure, to become metaphysicians, we must constantly return to the beginning spot and use repetition to resist the temptation constantly to rush forward to novelty.

To will repetition may at first seem to be the opposite of freedom. But either in its aesthetic employment when it creates novelty or in its ethical use to prove seriousness, S.K. wants to indicate how repetition leads to freedom. In the first place willing repetition demands a control over decision, so that it cannot be used by anyone except by conscious choice. We know that S.K. has denied that the past is any more necessary than the future, and repetition is a way of renewing the past with novelty. The greatest good which can be done for a being is to make him or her free, and S.K. is sure God has done this for us. In a fresh interpretation, he is sure that what originated through omnipotence can be independent. Usually God's creative power is thought to bind us up by necessity, but here S.K. reverses the doctrine and says that only omnipotence can withdraw itself and give away its power to determine.

The divine power and omnipotence are usually thought to be what require the predestination of human action, and S.K. often seems to agree to this traditional view of a God totally absorbed in eternal domination. Now, however, he reverses this and tells us that the art of power lies precisely in making another free. In this case, God's use of power leads to our freedom and not to our determination. God did not lose his power in creating man. He needs and preserves it all in order to make man independent. Some have wanted to compromise God's power in order to achieve human independence. S.K. thinks only God's full power can make man independent. To live independently is the most strenuous life, and Christianity, he feels, demands voluntariness.

Kierkegaard usually holds a very conservative picture of God, but he recognizes this by telling us he has a too mild conception of God. Yet the voluntary, which he senses in his own life, he thinks is too much for others to accept. This remark, if accepted, might lead us to think S.K.'s picture of God as eternal is more a nod to convention than a reflection of his own feelings. Yet freedom is not easy to get or to maintain. Only fear and trembling and constraint can help a man to freedom. So S.K.'s notions of freedom are certainly not the usual easy ones we associate with "being free." It is hard work and serious business, even for God.

If one argues in a scientific way with a phantom over whether one does or does not have freedom of choice, he may not notice that he has missed freedom. By staring fixedly at "freedom of choice" instead of choosing, he loses both freedom and freedom of choice. Freedom is essentially something to be demonstrated in choice. The greatest concession to man, S.K. says several times, is choice and freedom. The misuse of will is precisely what evil is. A man's choice becomes his fate, but one needs opposition and constraint to choose, not ease as we sometimes suppose. Thus, just as with "arguments" for the existence of God, S.K. feels arguments will not conclude the matter of freedom and may even be misleading. Freedom must be experienced in choice, but it can be found where the romantic least suspects it: in repetition properly handled and in the midst of great pressure—if it is properly met.

Self/God

Of all the contral concepts in S.K.'s thought, the "self" is perhaps both the most difficult and the most important. First of all, this is due to the importance of S.K.'s own relationship to his writings and the central place he gives to his personal life as an author. And the book's relationship to each reader is equally crucial. S.K. stops in one of his attacks and interjects, "if I may be permitted a word about myself." At this point the reader is ready to scream. S.K.'s concentration upon the self, both the reader's and his own, has been unremitting in all his writings, except perhaps in the aesthetic works which are intentionally "light" and not self-reflective. At the end of his career, S.K.'s intensity of self-concentration seems to reach a zenith, and his *Point of View* reintroduces the question of his relationship to his work in a new and perplexing way.

The *Journals,* of course, and all of the miscellaneous writings collected in his *Papers* reflect S.K.'s constant preoccupation with analyzing his professional task in relation to himself. This habit is not unconnected to his doctrine of the nature of the "self." It is part of his theory that the self is formed or understood only by constant reflection on its work and the insight which this ex post facto reflection yields. S.K.'s idea of the self as it emerges would not be what it is if it were not for the way in which he comes to understand his own role as an author. His works are so written that they involve the reader by requiring him to establish his own personal connection to the written works. And that is how S.K. thinks it should be.

Probably more people either react to or reject outright Kierkegaard as a philosopher because they disagree with his subjective and personal mode of dealing with most problems. Conversely, those who are attracted to S.K. are largely drawn because this puzzle over the subjective involvement of reader-with-author-with work seems to be illuminating. You cannot approach S.K.'s doctrine of the self without facing—or trying to face—its author, and readers are divided between finding this either a fascinating or an appalling way to do philosophy. Thus, S.K.'s views on the self also define what he thinks both philosophy and the religious life should be. If the self must be approached as S.K. says it must, philosophy is more than an academic enterprise. It requires a constant self-analysis.

Of course, we also face the problem of S.K.'s works which were published under pseudonyms. Even before he publically listed himself as their author, it was popularly known that S.K. was the responsible source. Yet somehow the indirection and the distance created or symbolized by the use of pseudonyms was important to his intentions as an author. Speaking directly is not always an appropriate approach for an author. This necessity for indirect communication is important if we want to understand the self and why it needs to be protected from a frontal approach. Later on S.K. will change and "speak out" directly. But by and large, he moves around his target rather than approaching it broadside. The self must be directed to itself and not allowed to direct attention outside of itself to the source of the words impinging upon it.

S.K. takes Socrates as his philosophical hero, because both he and Socrates make the quest for self-knowledge the center of their life and work. This cannot be assumed to be the automatic goal of everyone, because not all philosophers see their technical work as revolving around this aim. S.K.'s first work, *The Concept of Irony,* is replete with references about knowing the self or becoming self-transparent, and of course the subject of his essay is Socratic "irony." Evidently understanding irony is a key in the search for self-knowledge, and S.K. begins there rather than on some religious theme. He is trying to pull away from the Hegelian notion of the self, and Socratic irony provides him with the needed distance. Selfishness is that which needs to be overcome, if the self is to be changed, and S.K. begins with the premise that selves are made not born. We are not given a self; it is our project; it is the result of our activity. Thus, overcoming selfish attachment to the world and a desire to maintain spontaneity will block achievement in the popular, sophisticated sense, since it keeps one a child until this goal is accomplished.

"It is much easier to look to the right and to the left than to look into oneself" (*Thoughts on Crucial Situations,* trans. David Swenson, Minneapolis: Augsburg, 1941). However, S.K. suggests that the existential stress on death (p. 99) will make you unrecognizable to yourself for the present. This may set in motion the quest to learn to know yourself. Whether or not there is a real difference between S.K.'s Christian or edifying discourses and his other works, the question of the self looms large in both. It is obvious that the self is central as a religious problem or topic, and S.K. makes the self, its knowing and its change, crucial for philosophical thought too. His discourse (sermon) on "The Anxiety of Self-Torment" in *Christian Discourses* (trans. Walter Lowrie, Princeton University Press, 1971) is an example of the unavoidability of self-torment and its inescapable value for achieving understanding. It is the future which is disquieting, and our inability to live solely in the present is one source of our torment.

For Self-Examination, of course, takes this process as its explicit theme (trans. Walter Lowrie, Princeton University Press, 1944). If we are condemned, we often are self-condemned (p. 13). A little self-denial is the main thing Christianity requires, so that real understanding of the self involves the loss of self-concentration, not an increase. Yet "every man who carries out a true act of self-sacrifice will live to suffer for it" (p. 213). This indicates the way in which S.K. takes suffering to be an avenue to self-knowledge.

Constantly considering new probabilities leads away from discovering the deeper self. To lose oneself in knowing, to forget oneself in thinking or in artistic production, actually causes us to learn more about the deeper self. You can lose yourself in the knowledge of something else, but you can not do this when you come to know yourself before God (p. 122). There we must see ourselves directly and clear, or else God will elude us. In *Training in Christianity* (trans. Walter Lowrie, Princeton University Press, 1933), S.K. asks what it means to "draw to itself" (p. 159). He answers that it is to help to become oneself with and by the drawing into oneself. Drawing truly to oneself opens up a freedom which is involved in choice and in self-knowledge.

Since for S.K. self-denial is the meaning of being a Christian (p. 216), the central task is to know the self so that its demands can be set aside. Self-love, then, is a stumbling block. Self-torture is also our common lot, but the issue is whether or not it cures us of our self-love. It should give us an ability to achieve free decision focused outside the self. Yet, in order to understand sin, for example, we are always driven back to the meaning of self (*The Concept of Dread,* trans. Walter Lowrie, Princeton University Press, 1957). "If one does not first make clear to oneself what 'self' means, there is not much use of saying of sin that it is selfishness" (p. 70). "The real self is posited in the qualitative leap" (p. 71). Suffering is not simply self-torture (*Concluding Unscientific Postscript,* trans. David Swenson and Walter Lowrie, Princeton University Press, 1944), since suffering is the way of expressing existentially the task of dying away from immediacy. This is something which religiously must be done (p. 414), since the self is not discoverable in immediacy.

"To become conscious of oneself . . . is more significant than anything else in the world" (*Either/Or,* Vol. II., trans. Walter Lowrie, Princeton University Press, 1971, p. 210). But self-determination is a difficult business. This is particularly true in philosophy because it concentrates on thinking, whereas the self can be determined only by choice and action. S.K. asks, "What is this self of mine?" and he answers, "It is the most abstract of all things, and yet at the same time, it is the most concrete—it is freedom" (p. 218). You do not create yourself, but you do choose yourself.

It is a man's true salvation to be led into despair, since, although it is not pleasant, "despair is an experience which infinitizes" (p. 225). It is this lifting of the soul above itself which is necessary. The desired self is not an abstract self, which fits everywhere and hence nowhere. It is "a concrete self which stands in reciprocal relations with these surroundings, these conditions of life, this natural order" (p. 267). Decision making is presented as the key to structuring the self, to making it real in relation to its surroundings and itself. This power of decisiveness is, then, the secret of forming a self. Yet perhaps it is true that he who has not suffered does not know what decisiveness is, at least that kind which makes the self more and more concrete.

Of course, the focus of S.K.'s discussion of the problems of the self and its formation becomes evident in the difficult opening passages of *Sickness Unto Death* (trans. Walter Lowrie, Princeton University Press, 1954). Despair is a sickness in the spirit, in the self, he tells us. It is to this sickness that Christianity addresses itself, and it attempts to aid the self in discovery and in achieving wholeness (p. 146). Since despair comes because of not having a self one can call his own, its cure lies in the formation of a self with its own integrity. But what is the self? "The self is a relation which relates itself to its own self" *(ibid.)*, S.K. tells us in an enigmatic phrase.

Why is such self-relation necessary? Because man is an achieved synthesis, not a given substance. He must make a synthesis of the finite and the infinite, of the temporal and eternal, of freedom and necessity. These tend, when left to themselves, to split apart. The self is achieved when man holds together what otherwise would not remain in a unity. The individual relates to God in his aspect of infinity, but this clashes with the individual's finite side. We live in time, and yet we can transcend it. We know what eternity means. We can be governed by necessity as physical nature is, and in part we are. Yet we also can achieve free action, although none of these are easy to hold together. Thus, forming the self involves suffering.

The human self is a derived, constituted relation. Since the relation itself becomes a third thing, this eliminates forever any possibility of completeness in the self or in self-knowledge. Yet in relating itself to itself, the self relates itself to another. Although this overcomes isolation, it also introduces the necessity of knowing others as we know ourself. The self cannot attain and remain in equilibrium and rest on its own, and this is the source of one form of our despair. Sometimes it does not will to be itself, and that is another source of the self's despair. However, the most difficult source of despair to deal with is the fact that the source of the self's desired equilibrium lies outside of itself.

As is well known, S.K. introduces God as the Power which can ground the self (p. 147). In doing so he follows a long tradition in theology, although he does this in his own unique way. The path of interior exploration leads eventually to God, and we discover God as the model for the self and its own hope for a rest in its flight. S.K.'s doctrine of God is not systematically developed. At times God's nature becomes radically like man's experience, but in this instance God retains a classical serenity and repose. He is described as the power man needs. By willing to be himself, man finds himself transparently grounded in the power which posited him. The struggle of the self with itself leads, knowingly or unknowingly, into the arms of God.

Sometimes we have thought of the individual's perfect qualities as those which make him like God and place him above the beasts, but S.K. says that it is his openness to the sickness of despair which elevates man. This sickness proves his relation to infinity, so that our human disproportion is never healed because the synthesis of finite and infinite can never be stable beyond the moment. Yet to be able to despair is an advantage. It shows the constant presence of possibility as well as actuality. If he were not a synthesis, man could not despair, so "this thing of despairing is inherent in man himself" (p. 149). Without it man might not know God, for despair is related to the eternal in man, and it is this which enables him to discover his hidden core.

"The torment of despair is precisely this, not to be able to die" (p. 250). That is what it means for the self to be "sick unto death": not to be able to die. The dying of despair thus transforms itself constantly into living, precisely because despair is self-consuming and yet never completes its task. Despair would get rid of the self it does not want, but instead it breeds further despair "because he cannot consume himself, cannot get rid of himself, cannot become nothing" (p. 151). To be compelled to be a self one does not will to be is our torment, namely, that we cannot get rid of that self. If the process of discovering the self were any less difficult, despair would be less prominent.

At the same time despair discloses the eternal in man; in the biblical phrase: "And the bush was not consumed." What should destroy him does not. Man would not despair if he did not have something of the eternal in him. He would live happily in the moment. What he despairs of is achieving the synthesis set as a goal for him, but he also discovers that despair does not put an end to the matter, that he lives on. When this happens, he discovers the eternal, the indestructible side of himself without which he would have perished in despair long ago and given up his project to achieve a self. "To have a self, to be a self, is the greatest concession made to man, but at the same time it is eternity's demand upon him" (p. 154).

The sickness of the self takes many forms, as S.K. outlines them, and these can also be dealt with in many ways. However, the curing of souls is the main business of man and of religion. There is no higher synthesis he can pass on to or hope for as an end. The self *is* this struggle. It need not miss all happiness or be entirely overcome by despair, but the basic disproportion remains constantly there. Man cannot be part divine and have it otherwise. If he runs from his sickness and covers it over with pleasure, he misses his opportunity to form the relation which constitutes the full self. He can accept the challenge and God's presence and his assigned part. The self is not thereby constituted to all eternity, but at least we know what the problem is and how it can and cannot be dealt with.

As indicated above, Kierkegaard is quite traditional and conservative when it comes to his view of God's nature, except for an occasional radical suggestion made in passing. But it is interesting to review every mention S.K. makes in his writing about God. When you do you see that, except for a few major exceptions (e.g., *Fear and Trembling, Sickness Unto Death, Philosophical Fragments*), S.K. speaks about God primarily in religious vs. theological terms. Luther and the Bible are mentioned often, and the themes are repentance, love, and majesty. For all his individualism and democratic spirit, Kierkegaard still speaks of God primarily in kingly terms and in majestic images. God suffers little of the anguish which becomes so normative for man under the existential analysis.

God does not change; man changes his position in relation to God —which is a rather traditional view. But S.K. does speak with great familiarity about God, so that it is hard to believe the sometimes mentioned assertion that S.K. is himself a disbeliever. To relate to God is an excruciating task that never allows man to rest, but S.K. is constantly working at it. He rejects any man trying to create God in his own image. S.K.'s God is a majestic, transcendent, and even terrifying figure. But the picture is paradoxically mixed, for love and forgiveness are there, too. God is able to forget man's sins, S.K. tells us in one very human image of God's actions. God is simultaneously far and near. That is the dilemma man must deal with, and to become a self demands that he do just this.

S.K. does not waste time "proving" God's existence. Belief in God is a matter of commitment, not logic. People, and particularly priests, are always trying to pull God down to their level and domesticate him, but S.K. rejects all this with a passion. To love God is to be happy at the same time that the experience is terrifying. Becoming involved with God, which it is clear Kierkegaard is, launches you on a spiritual trial. Yet only the God-relationship gives the individual significance, he asserts, which makes trying to face God crucial for defining an authentic self. You suffer at the hands of God and yet relate yourself to him as child to father. A man needs the help of a community, but for S.K. facing God is essentially a lonely, individual task. God is a God of love, but he demands obedience. Man is caught between these two poles.

We must think humanly about God and yet not compromise his infinite sublimity. God is revealed and yet he is still hidden. He creates us separate, and yet creation is fulfilled only when God is included in it. To become involved with God is almost beyond human strength and endurance, but the springs lie within for one who can learn to turn inward to God. God is gentle and patient. But life with God is also strenuous, and he knows suffering. God is not interested in established religious orders, but we are, due to our frailty. God is too much to bear alone. The closer you come to God the more rigorous he becomes. A mediation is necessary (although we must note that S.K. seldom speaks of this) due to God's aloofness.

Suffering comes from God, S.K. is sure. The more an individual is involved with God, the more difficulties enter his life. Suffering and misfortune actually signify God's love, and there is obedience due absolute majesty. God has only one passion: to love and to be loved. God loves and he wants to be loved. God is a majesty embattled with the devil, S.K. says in traditional imagery. And there is only one thing to do about God's majesty: worship him. God is at one and the same time infinitely close to man and infinitely far away. As is clear, S.K. is radical in his philosophical and psychological suggestions but follows Luther closely in matters of theology. God is personal, but you cannot tell if he will be personal for you. That depends on his pleasure.

It is not possible to approach God directly, and long ago humanity ceased to be able to bear the pressure and weight of a personal God. As we grow soft and weak, we reject God implicitly, because we make it impossible for ourselves to relate to such a being. God sits in heaven and waits for someone to become involved with him, but today we have a sense of God's withdrawal only because we have grown too weak to meet the challenge of becoming involved. To constitute a strong, independent self is a hard task that never ends, and so is relating oneself to God. The two tasks are joined together, because both ultimately are as demanding and worthwhile as they are difficult. God is eternal, and these problems of relationship are man's eternal projects.

Subjective/Suffering

Even for such a strange thinker as Kierkegaard, it may seem odd to pair such concepts as "subjective" and "suffering." Of course, S.K. is largely responsible for making "subjective" famous in the existential vocabulary, but it is usually paired with its opposite, "objective." It should be, and I will present it that way. But a little more careful examination of S.K.'s use reveals an interesting connection of "subjective" with "suffering." Since "subjective" may be S.K.'s most popular and most used term, it would pay us to find a new approach which would make clear the special stress he gives to this term. Of course, in his aggravating way, S.K. never really intends to give precise and single definitions to his central terms. That would defeat his purpose of forcing the reader to do this for himself.

Subjective is often taken in an extreme meaning, such as S.K.'s claim that all that matters is the subjective passion and inwardness with which an individual adopts or identifies himself with an idea. This of course most primarily refers to the doctrines of Christianity as he outlines these in *Concluding Unscientific Postscript.* These are contrasted with the objective uses of theological dogma and are related to his assertion that "objectively" Christianity has no existence. First, we have to recognize that S.K. does not deny that people can be listed on the roles of churches which are called Christian and therefore be designated as such. He simply wants to underline his conviction that the heart and whole purpose of Christ's mission lies in inducing passionate acceptance, and then action, on the part of individuals.

As with most of the confusion we have in trying to understand S.K., the problem with subjectivity arises because S.K. himself often speaks of it in the extreme, that is, as if passion is all that mattered. To emphasize the importance of the subjective appropriation, he often does talk in extreme terms. Yet in many places, including the *Post-script,* it is clear that subjectivity never stands alone; in fact it cannot. There can be no such thing as blind subjective appropriation. First, an objective issue must be proposed; for instance, Jesus was born at such and such a time and place and came to represent God to us. Objective issues pose the problem first and they remain, but S.K. wants to stress that some—not all—problems are false if left on a purely objective level. Particularly in the case of Christianity, the dual aspects of the issue and the subjective appropriation demanded must both be stressed.

Because existence demands decisiveness, the stress on subjectivity is demanded so that all existence does not dissolve into indifferent talk about "matters of fact." Some issues involve our existence; they must be approached as such, and then finally adopted or rejected with passion. Of course, S.K. has a hidden premise here which is that in important cases, particularly Christianity, objective treatment of the facts can never be sufficient to yield a personal decision. Yet if S.K. seems to assume this irreducible indeterminancy of certain crucial issues, his opponents (the advocates of a purely objective determination of all issues) usually assume that all of life's issues are decidable objectively without the subjective addition of human passion.

Every human being is a subject, and it is important to recognize that one runs a risk in any resolution or decision of choice. Of course, advocates of objective determination usually assume all issues are resolveable in a final and conclusive manner. But S.K.'s message is that some issues are not subject to such certainty, and so they always force the element of risk on the human being who does not run away from them. But it is not easy. The whole issue must first be worked through thoroughly. Hasty and impulsive decisions are not S.K.'s aim. Subjectivity raises the issues of inwardness, of individual spirit and freedom. That is why to avoid all subjectivity by trying to decide the issue always on an objective plane is to eliminate much that is important to the human being. But all this is difficult to grasp and it cannot be hastily done.

Primarily the difficulty comes about because these issues, e.g., living out Christian preaching, bring us to wrestle with God alone, and that involves risk. This lonely battle of the human spirit with God is the same from age to age and does not change from the time of the Apostles until now. That is, its resolution lies on the level of subjective deepening, not on the level of scientific advance. Objectivity, in fact, is often an excuse to avoid the demand to sacrifice individuality. Here is the first connection of subjectivity to suffering, but it does not color all problems. The task is to be objective toward oneself and subjective toward others. Subjectivity is not license for an excess of personal concentration. There is Christian doctrine (objectivity) and then there is the matter of interiorizing it by giving it power in one's life (subjectivity).

To avoid decision, people equivocate by talking objectively. In religious terms, the sin is to be objective, that is, to turn outward instead of inward. Objectivity has slipped in to separate the individual from facing God, and sin means to avoid God. S.K. does not deny the Lutheran doctrine of salvation by grace alone, but we become fatalistic unless we accept the fact that there is something each individual can do and must do about becoming a believer. There are a multitude of important objective problems, but in the case of both ethics and religion the issue is to realize these existentially in the lives of the individuals. God realized his doctrine in the incarnation by actually becoming man, and, as far as Christianity goes, it is every individual's task to realize doctrine in this same concrete way.

Kierkegaard has a nack of putting simple truths in a graphic but perhaps difficult manner, and it is his intention to do so to get our attention and to make us struggle to understand. You can say that "subjectivity" simply refers to the relation between doctrine and human existence. That probably is correct, but it misses part of S.K.'s intention by making the point so easy that it is also easy to avoid. Some philosophers want to remove difficulties; S.K. wants to create them, but only at the points where men escape decision and uncertainty and facing God alone by accepting solutions too quickly. Your life should guarantee what you say, and S.K. wants to point to the necessity of more than verbal resolution when ethics and religion are concerned. It is inconvenient to be committed and men naturally want to escape. However, it is the philosopher's job not just to clarify language but also to force the individual to his own life enactment.

Most people are afraid to look at themselves, S.K. is convinced, and so they avoid subjective examination by claiming all problems can be objectively determined. In a sense they can be, for all issues involve certain matters of fact which can be objectively discussed. It is just that certain important issues require individual appreciation where finality is not possible and risk is unavoidable. Christianity can be taught objectively and heard objectively, but this brings us only to what S.K. calls "Christiandom" (its formal side) vs. individual Christianity. S.K. also offers the interesting insight that, as long as we do not appropriate Christianity personally, it will look like only poetry and mythology. Held away from the individual objectively, it is bound to appear that way, but it changes when appropriated subjectively.

It is helpful to see what S.K. wants to say in his doctrine of "subjectivity" if we compare it with his almost constant reference to suffering. The important point is not his preoccupation with his own suffering but to see how subjective appropriation involves a suffering that objective appropriation avoids. Decisiveness in relation to crucial but indeterminate questions is impossible to achieve without the changes induced by the experience of suffering. To be spared suffering is to lose all personal decisiveness, and certainly suffering is for S.K. the chief byproduct of individual relationship to God. A life that is too happy avoids suffering, but it also lacks all basis to relate to God. One does not simply decide to face hard decisions subjectively. Enduring suffering forms our spirit into one which is able to decide, if the suffering is religiously appropriated.

Of course, the reader doesn't have to read S.K.'s words about suffering very long before he realizes that S.K. is a romantic. Adversity always unites people and brings about beautiful inner community, he is sure; he doesn't seem to see the destructive and devastating side of suffering. Man invented laughter; crying is a divine gift, he is also sure. Of course, suffering comes from the relationship to God. To know God and not to suffer is impossible. But the Christian is one who freely chooses suffering when he could avoid it. This again is the relationship of subjectivity to suffering. Objectively, suffering can often be avoided, but not in subjective appropriation or nearness to God. Christianity is never "true" in some objective situation. It only becomes so in choice and in the experience of suffering, which is just what total objectivity and non-involvement seek to avoid. Humanity seeks pleasure; suffering is a Christian duty.

Interestingly enough, on this interpretation suffering cannot be said to be a punishment for sin. It could be avoided by holding to objective detachment, but it is the result of a free decision to be committed personally and to become involved. S.K.'s theory, then, makes God responsible only for offering man the choice of commitment and involvement with God, which brings suffering as its result, not the necessary imposition of suffering on man. Of course, this only accounts for subjective suffering, the inner anguish which S.K. thinks most men fight to avoid. It is not an account of physical evil and destruction. As an anti-systematic theologian, S.K. does not directly develop an account of evil. But as a psychologist and analyst of religious consciousness, he points to the voluntary but fruitful appropriation of suffering as God-consciousness producing, which would seem to justify suffering as far as he is concerned.

The Kingdom of God cannot be brought on earth without tribulation, so the individual who relates to Christianity by subjective commitment cannot hope to be free of suffering. It is characteristic of the religious man to be an alien, to be an exile, so that to make Christianity too mild is to falsify it. We must suffer, in order to allow injustice to have its rights, but still to win over it. We cannot be ruthless against injustice, and yet it must be rooted out. To use fair means to do this is to suffer. It is a false church which persecutes; the true church is persecuted. We cannot seek assistance in our struggle from outside, because God has dictated that our relationship be to him alone. Unfortunately, suffering is intensified when it is voluntary, because it is painful to know we could avoid it but have elected not to.

Man and man may join together so as to eliminate suffering, but God and man cannot. Suffering is part of any God relationship. If you do not suffer, you have nothing to do with God. However, S.K. seems to think the ungodly are exempt from suffering, and that probably overstresses his point a bit. A spiritual being can perhaps be involved with God only if he suffers, but that does not necessarily mean that one who is not involved with God might not suffer too. S.K. wants to recognize God's grace in reverse, but that perhaps is to make the experience of grace too morbid rather than joyful. S.K. thinks that to be unhappy is a sign that God loves you, which may be partially true, but it does stress the morbid side a bit excessively.

S.K. clearly makes suffering the sign of a God relationship, but this is to put love on a rather negative plane. There is a need for the Christian to "die to the world," and suffering is a catalyst in the process. We must avoid loving God egotistically, simply because we think he favors us and learn to love God in adversity too, a lesson Job teaches us. Rather than morbidity, what S.K. wants to point out is that one must first die to the world before he can be happy in loving God, and our severance from the world involves suffering. Yet one does not ask for suffering (as S.K. seems to at times). You venture because you must, and then you accept the consequences without seeking them or predicting them. It is hard to endure suffering, but it is the transformation one should hope for.

S.K. does go too far when he equates love of God with hatred for the world. Some have thought it necessary to do that, but the Christian recommendation is more complex and less clear-cut. God does not hate our whole existence, as S.K. sometimes seems to suggest, but there are parts God enjoys and parts he condemns. S.K. goes so far as to say God has to suffer for human beings. That suggestion could lead to interesting consequences, but S.K. does not follow them up. He suggests rather than explores. Tranquility is not allowed to Christians. S.K. may overstate his position from time to time, but its aim is not to allow us to languish in a falsely tranquil notion of what Christianity demands of us.

Truth/Authority

In a real sense, the reader may view Kierkegaard's whole literary effort as an attempt to reach truth or to state truth. But S.K. has (or he develops) such a special view of what truth is that it is not easy to understand this at first. In fact, it is clear that S.K. himself is struggling to discover what truth is, how it is reached, and how it is or can be stated. Essentially, of course, what S.K. wants to endorse is an age-old distinction between "speaking the truth" and "living the truth." What complicates matters, however, is that truth is a minority affair and cannot be understood by majorities. Thus S.K. is not a "democratic" in the simple meaning of that term, or at least he is not where Christianity and living out its injunctions are concerned. However, it does not follow that minority views are always right, either. Truth is less easy to pin down than that.

Like the relation of suffering to subjectivity, S.K. believes truth must suffer to prove its validity. An easy truth would be a contradiction in terms. He is so absorbed in the notion of suffering that he thinks truth is identified by the fact that it suffers. He sides against the establishment, too, and finds more "truth" in the fallacies of sects than in the drowsiness of the established religions. By that, of course, he means they are more courageous and act out their faith rather than quietly confessing it in well-worn words. Truth does not rule the world, because men avoid suffering if they can. One must set himself apart to become aware of truth, and few can accept such loneliness.

Since we can not gain truth by group effort, it involves the loneliness of isolation. Thus it also brings up S.K.'s favorite image, the "single individual." This is the only way to explore truth, but it is a lonely path. One has to give up much, and few are willing to risk that "lonesome road." Thus, truth is a complex concept. And for S.K. it is linked to many of his pet issues, but one key link is to "authority." S.K. likes paradoxical links, and so to stress individual loneliness and still make a place for authority in truth pulls opposites together in a way that intrigues S.K. One is on his own, and yet there is an authority which must be obeyed. Of course, the authority is not human in origin but only from God, so the issue is to distinguish human authority from God's. S.K. devotes a whole book to *Authority and Revelation*. For all his stress on the need for passion and subjectivity, there is a norm to conform to—if we can find it.

Anyone who discovers divine authority can venture further out than the ordinary man, but the problem always is: How can divine teaching enter into a prosaic world? Obedience is the response to authority, so that S.K. tempers his advice for individual rebellion with a counsel to obey. But the issue is how the individual can know when that time has come. Christianity first came to us substantiated by authority, but the issue is how to recognize that source today. Thus S.K.'s whole literary effort is a quest to establish how and whether it is still possible to recover an original authority. It has been done. Christianity was established. Socrates did teach, but the issue is to repeat the same search in each new day.

Witness/Apostle

The twin concepts which go with Truth/Authority are Witness/Apostle. These illustrate the basic theme of S.K.'s work and also the tensions in it. It is not enough to find the truth in individual search and suffering. It must be witnessed to or else it is not alive. Truth is something to be done. God is still the source of truth, but that is all the more reason it requires suffering and action. And a witness is different from a teacher. A teacher presents; a witness testifies himself. He directly demonstrates in his life the truth of the doctrine he presents, whereas the teacher need have no such relationship to what he expounds. The teacher has proofs and arguments, but, by design, he himself stands outside of them. Christianity demands witnesses, but the teacher is more of a poet and stage-player.

Of course, a witness to the truth as a speaker is not as eloquent. That is not his function. Shrewdness is something different, too. What is needed is simple action. A final unconditional venture is required, and this cannot be taught. Thus, S.K. joins Plato and Augustine in maintaining the basic "inteachability" of truth, but the important point is that it can be witnessed to. Teachers live by becoming actors. Witnesses are all-consuming. Thus, many shy from becoming a witness and prefer the role of a teacher, because it is more comfortable and less demanding. But the world is not advanced in this way, or at least Christianity is not, no matter how much is learned about it by various professions. Witnessing is another matter.

What S.K. has in mind here is his "ultimate category," the "apostle." In philosophical terms, he has come to teach us about the individual. In religious terms, he has come to preach to us about the apostle. To be an apostle is not the high honor one usually talks about. We may look at it that way in retrospect, after the patina of history has glossed over the loneliness, uncertainty, and suffering involved. To be an apostle is sheer earthly suffering, and we are prone to forget that. While he is living, to call himself an apostle does not help him gain honor, respect, or advantage. In fact, the opposite is true. We forget this hard fact because we grant the apostle honor, not at the time but in retrospect. It is hard to find one who can stand the persecution involved, and yet, in looking back and writing about the past, we act as if history is full of such men and women.

Christianity is not a doctrine but a way of existence. What it needs is not professors but witnesses. Jesus did not need scholars but was satisfied with fishermen. And we talk of Christianity as if it did not involve us, but one cannot speak of Christianity at all without perpetual self-accusation. That is, the only way to speak of it in truth is to become a witness, and that is not to juggle words but to indicate one's willingness to live the life of an apostle. If we don't, to speak of Christianity is not to accuse others but ourselves. To live such a life is to put oneself out of the understanding of most men. It is clear that Kierkegaard did this and still does this today to his readers. It is also true that, when S.K. lashes out at others, he is primarily berating himself, demanding that his life somehow live up to the words he writes about it.

Retrospective Summary

"Kierkegaard is a dangerous man," said a friend of mine following a discussion about that controversial author. It is easy to imagine that Søren Kierkegaard would have relished such a comment, since he did everything in his writing to make it impossible for us to assimilate his essays without caution. Kierkegaard cannot be read either easily or lightly, and that is the way he wanted it to be. Time and again he tells us that each reader must work out his own solution. He uses his author's bag of tricks, not to reach a conclusion, but simply to make each reader become aware. We are to be ever on the alert and never at rest.

It is impossible to be a reader of Kierkegaard very long without the impression that the author is laughing at you at times, defying you to believe him if you can. Then, suddenly, he will switch to some serious point, leaving no absolute line of demarcation between the supercilious and the profound. Kierkegaard speaks time and again about the difficult relationship of author to reader. When he raises this issue, we should always listen carefully. It is the only basis upon which to understand the flood of writing he produced. Two of his own comments on authorship are crucial:

> . . . an author . . . who writes in order to be misunderstood, . . . to count it to his credit that Professor Heiberg had not understood him (*The Concept of Dread,* trans. Walter Lowrie, Princeton Univ. Press, 1946, p. 17).

> . . . an author who, so far as I am acquainted with him, is sometimes rather deceitful—not, however in such a way that he

might say one thing and mean another, but in such a way that he carries the thought to extremes, so that, if it is not grasped with the same energy, it appears the next moment to be something different (*Repetition,* trans. Walter Lowrie, Princeton Univ. Press, 1946, p. 6).

In reading, one must match Kierkegaard's own energy in writing, or all hope of understanding is lost.

We need to be on guard against the "tricks" Kierkegaard may play upon his readers. Even more, we need to resist any dogmatic or final interpretation given to us of Kierkegaard's views. This includes S.K.'s own self-interpretation. He warned us that his successors would make a mockery of his words by giving them an overly scholarly treatment, one which would claim to explain all his thought in some synthesis. Time and again he writes parodies on pedantic inquiry which thinks a little more research can yield a final answer.

It is a touch of irony that his own words have been transformed into finished doctrines in precisely the manner he gave his energy to prevent. Thus, S.K. denies that a system is possible where men are concerned. It ought not to be possible to "systematize" his own writings. This holds true in spite of the fact that he contradicted himself by offering his own self-summary in his last days (see *Point of View*). The only interpretation of Kierkegaard which should be rejected, then, is one which claims authority and finality for itself.

Our problem in hermenutics is that we are dealing with an author who: (1) insisted on the importance of his personal life for his writings, (2) left us a journal which may be as much poetry as fact, (3) denied the possibility of uncovering a final solution that would piece all the views together, (4) at the same time he produced his own interpretive key to his writings, (5) but the key which he gave us is neither entirely consistent nor fully adequate to cover the whole authorship. Certain decisive transformations take place during the period of his writing. Whether they are precisely as he describes them and whether they have the significance he and others attach to them—this is the dialectical issue which each reader must face individually.

It is necessary to enter into combat with S.K. over his own interpretation. One question is whether *Authority and Revelation* provides a valuable and perhaps revolutionary clue. What would happen, we ask, if we look at Kierkegaard's collected works using *Authority and*

Revelation as an alternative to his own self-conscious "point of view"? There is some evidence that this might be a valuable thing to do. Clearly S.K. changes in his later days, although understanding the nature of this change is the question at issue.

In 1846 the first copy of what he called *The Book on Adler* was finished, but he did not publish it. This is the year in which the *Concluding Unscientific Postscript* was completed. The authorship which was to have ended now suddenly begins again on a new key. He publicly acknowleges the pseudonymous works as his own. He announces a decisive change in himself and begins to speak directly. He starts the fantastic controversy with *The Corsair* which dominates the later years of his life. What did the discoveries S.K. made as he wrote about Adler have to do with all this? Why did this manuscript remain, together with *The Point of View,* unpublished until after his death?

The Point of View shares a similar history, but it has been accepted as accounting for the decisive changes is S.K.'s life. It is taken as the perspective within which we can understand Kierkegaard's authorship as a whole. It is his own direct account, it is true. Yet he has warned us time and again that indirect techniques are the only authentic means, that direct statements are a necessary deception which stand in need of careful correction. Let us accept S.K.'s oft-given advice and remain skeptical of even his own direct summary.

Let us try an experiment which applies S.K.'s analysis of Adler to Kierkegaard himself and to his works. *The Book on Adler* comes at a crucial period in S.K.'s productive life and has fascinating circumstances surrounding it. At least it must be taken with greater seriousness than it usually has been. To accomplish this: First, an account of the important themes in *Authority and Revelation;* then, a brief review of S.K.'s writings to see what light is shed by applying S.K.'s words on Adler to Kierkegaard himself.

I
The Individual

Before turning to appraise any single work, we must first pay attention to Kierkegaard himself. The one thing he never lets the reader forget is S.K. Whether or not we accept his own particular interpretation of the relation between an author and his writing, we are forced to consider this issue. S.K. himself has raised it so many times. Romantic exaggeration is present whenever Kierkegaard speaks about himself, so it is quite possible that the personal element has been overstressed. Nevertheless, it is there.

This personal, self-referential element is inescapable. It is said that the story of his life is the story of his authorship, but that is too easy and too obvious a view of which we must beware. First, we should ask: what do we mean by "the story of his life"? If we mean his own words, written in his *Journals* (which he wrote expressly for publication) and elsewhere, then we must ask whether his own account is prosaic fact or more like romantic poetry.

His short life, if inwardly stormy, was outwardly rather quiet and comfortable. His father was a wealthy merchant who left Kierkegaard well provided for. He never needed to work to earn his living during his lifetime and he never did. Copenhagen at his time had a conservative and traditional society, and S.K. left its security for only a few short trips. Inside Denmark he was a well-regarded and famous figure, known to the Danish royalty and conversant with every famous figure of his day.

Marx was writing *The Communist Manifesto* during this same period S.K. wrote *Works of Love*. But, if Kierkegaard rebelled along with Marx, it was an inner not an outer rebellion, which befits his own stress on inwardness. Kierkegaard lived, if not in splendor, at least in solid comfort, until he had exhausted his inheritance near the end of his life. He did not teach; he did not preach. He talked increasingly about becoming a country parson, but he never did. He did write, and his writings have had great impact, but his own life was not particularly outgoing. He complained of being a genius in a provincial town, but he enjoyed the esteem and flattery that go with such a situation.

Except as his writing brought him into the public view, Kierkegaard did not lead an active life. In his later years he asked for and got a public storm unleashed upon him. He attacked Bishop Mynster, an old family friend, after the respected bishop's death, and all over a reference in Bishop Martensen's funeral oration which named the late bishop a "witness to the truth." Kierkegaard thereupon unleashed his attack in public on the late and revered bishop, and also upon the church. This was only one of the violent outbursts which marked his last years. The church stood in need of a challenge, but the occasion of the attack seems hardly rational. One interesting fact concerning *Authority and Revelation* is that it was Bishop Mynster who suspended Adler from his pastoral duties, charging that his mind was deranged.

S.K.'s public and violent denial of Bishop Mynster's right to be called a "witness to the truth" came after his book on Adler. The more famous controversy with *The Corsair* came just as the *Postscript* was finished and Adler was on Kierkegaard's mind. *The Corsair* was a controversial political journal given to attacks upon the establishment. However, S.K. was the one prominant figure the editor (Goldschmidt) did not abuse, due to his respect for Kierkegaard. S.K. demanded that he be included in their ridicule, but he had to reveal the connection of P. L. Möller with *The Corsair* to force them to do so. Möller wanted a university chair, but Kierkegaard's public revelation of his secret editorial connection with this questionable journal ruined the man's career. He soon left the country, a finished man. S.K. got the abuse he asked for, although for the most part it was simply caricature. However, he had to destroy another man's career in order to receive any treatment worth complaining about.

He died having spent his father's fortune. He refused on his deathbed to be reconciled with his brother. He attacked a family friend after his death over a statement made in eulogy of the departed. Still, he succeeded in attracting to himself nothing but respect, except for forcing a public attack upon himself at the expense of another man's career. All this does not detract from S.K.'s genuine religious insight or psychological profundity, although it does tell us something about the religious personality. It forces us to distinguish, on S.K.'s own terms, the outer from the inner.

Outwardly, S.K. had little to complain about, except what he brought upon himself. Inwardly, he was torn, but to try to understand the inner Kierkegaard as he emerged on paper by reference to the outer circumstances is to misunderstand the man's words on the subject, although he is partly responsible for the confusion in this matter. He had so little to complain about that he was forced to provide his own grounds for complaint.

By way of contrast, A.P. Adler (1812–69) was a priest on the Island of Bornholm who, although an intellectual, was well loved by the parish. S.K. talked often of becoming just such a country parson and intended to end his writing career to do this the year in which he wrote *The Book on Adler*. But in fact he never did. Unlike S.K., Adler was highly addicted to Hegel, as was Bishop Martensen. Adler based his writing upon a claim to special revelation, and this claim was on S.K.'s mind during the time he felt he, too, had undergone a decisive religious transformation. The striking parallels—and differences—could not have escaped Kierkegaard, and perhaps they account for his intense interest in Adler. The suspension of Adler from his priesthood was a minor affair, but in this minor incident S.K. may have learned more about himself than in the conscious attempt to write his own *Point of View*.

II
"The Book on Adler"

Our task is to set down the insights which, according to Kierkegaard, Adler's case produced for him. Then we can compare these with the central doctrines in S.K.'s other writings. The reader must decided whether this encounter with Adler unintentionally provides an insight into S.K. himself and his total authorship. Kierkegaard's uncertainty over publishing this manuscript, its many drafts and numerous prefaces, its timing at a transitional period in S.K.'s writing, in the lull before the storm which he brought upon himself—this should move us to make a close analysis of this work for its possible disclosure at the moment of crisis. That is Kierkegaard's favorite situation to produce insight. It is an old saw that our criticisms of others tell as much about us as they do about their intended targets.

One way to see the radical impact of the doctrines contained in *Authority and Revelation* is to consider what S.K. is saying if we knew only *A & R* and nothing of his other writings. We want to understand how S.K.'s earlier doctrines appear when considered from "the point of view" of *A & R*. Considered in isolation, the views of *A & R* yield a quite different Kierkegaard, just as we see a different man if we read S.K.'s devotional and purely religious writings, his edifying discourses.

The problem in understanding S.K. is to put all the perspectives together. But we must be cautious about assuming in advance that all the pieces may fit together into a consistent whole. That is, they may not be understandable on a single basis. Perhaps, as S.K. tells us, no synthesis is possible. If so, we have to remain skeptical of any "explanation" which claims to resolve every conflict into one resolution—including Kierkegaard's own. In understanding S.K., we must never allow our understanding to come to rest upon any one solution.

After completing the manuscript of *A & R* in one draft in 1846, Kierkegaard wrote two prefaces for it in the next year and a third, and longer one, in 1848. He tells us the book is intended for theologians, which is interesting since S.K. seldom wrote either formal theology or explicitly for theologians. Kierkegaard admits that Adler is the subject of the book only in the sense that his case throws light upon dogmatic concepts. He intends to pay as much attention to the age as to Adler. Kierkegaard intentionally is often a confusing writer, yet he begins by deploring Adler's "confusion" (p. xvi). He admits that Adler was just what he (S.K.) needed; Adler's going astray was very opportune.

"Revelation" is the subject of the book and that is interesting, because S.K. seldom paid much direct attention to it. When he did, as in the doctrine of the incarnation, he stressed its paradoxical nature, its total rational unassimilability. Revelation leaves man faced with the absurd as the only condition of his faith. Now S.K. says revelation suffers from confusion in his own age, and he equates the investigation of this with the concept of "authority" (p. xvi). If revelation had been considered heretofore only as it produced paradox, Keirkegaard hardly considered authority at all prior to this. It is at odds with S.K.'s constant stress upon the absolute aloneness of the *individual* in matters of faith. Kierkegaard says that the age has confused the concept of authority, but he himself almost ignored it up till now—until Adler "woke him from his individualistic slumbers."

S.K. declares that he has read and reread Adler's writings because they provide a transparent medium for seeing the confusion of his age. Kierkegaard claims that Christianity's greatest enemies are not those who are irreligious. We should be afraid of those who are under religious influence but who are also religiously confused. Previously S.K. stressed absolute individuality and complained about the lack of passion. Now he changes his analysis of the faults of his age:

> For the misfortune of our age . . . is disobedience, unwillingness to obey. And one deceives oneself and others by wishing to make us imagine that it is doubt. No, it is insubordination: it is not doubt of religious truth but insubordination against religious authority which is the fault in our misfortune and the cause of it.
> Disobedience is the secret of the religious confusion of our age. (p. xviii).

Reading this it is hard to remember that the author is the same man who always claims to be tormented by tremendous doubts and who constantly spoke of subjectivity and of anguish. Adler affected S.K., and he tells us that he had to "take a step backward to get the point of view" *(ibid)*. S.K. begs us to read his book on Adler, remembering that it is important to his main effort, but this importance has not always been discovered. It will be an edifying book, S.K. adds mysteriously, for him who understands it.

In the third preface, Kierkegaard speaks of Christianity as able to solve the problems of the age, whereas before Christianity was depicted as an utterly unsolvable problem itself. Christianity can explain in time what otherwise in the temporal order remains a riddle, S.K. now tells us. Of course, this is not a worldly understanding, and it does require a leap into the religious.

S.K. turns next to the concept of the martyr, which obsesses him in his last years. True martyrdom stems from obedience:

> And this sacrifice is the sacrifice of obedience, wherefore God looks with delight upon him, the obedient man, who offers himself as a sacrifice, whereas he gathers his wrath against disobedience which slays the sacrifice—this sacrifice, the victor, is the martyr; for not everyone who is put to death is a martyr (p. xxiv).

Ruling religiously is a form of punishment and involves suffering. However, Kierkegaard draws a very important distinction between selfish, self-induced suffering and suffering which is submissive, which does not seek its own ends:

> . . . in a *worldly* sense one makes a fuss over sufferings, one suffers in order to conquer—and then perhaps he doesn't conquer after all. In a Christian sense . . . he does not suffer in order to conquer, but rather because he has conquered, which simply gives him pleasure in putting up with everything and exalts him above sufferings, for once he has conquered he can surely put up with a bit of suffering (p. xxvi).

This is written by a man who spent his last years complaining loudly about the suffering he had to endure, by one who spent most of his life feeling sorry for himself in print. This indeed is a new maturity Adler has induced, but it did not prevent S.K.'s exaggerated final acts. To see and to do are not the same, and Kierkegaard closes his preface by once again proclaiming that he himself is "without authority."

Producing books does not make a man an author, S.K. reports. An author should be able to complete his work, and yet the last part cannot be written. If he goes ahead and writes the last part (as S.K. did in the *Point of View*), "he will make it thoroughly clear by writing the last part that he makes a written remunciation to all claim to be an author" (pp. 3–4). A genuine author knows that no project can really be finished and completed and placed in final perspective. To find a conclusion really means to discover that one is lacking and to feel this lack keenly. "Every poetic conclusion is an illusion" (p. 4). This statement comes at a time when S.K. is preoccupied with an authorship he intended to leave incomplete with the publication of the *Postscript.* But he reversed himself and added his own conclusion.

Kierkegaard now begins his important analysis of the "premise-author" vs. the "essential author." The former is outer directed, the latter is inner directed. The premise-author tries to raise an outcry. He thinks this a good thing for its own sake, but he must wait for something outside himself to enlighten him. He needs to communicate, and if he has great talents he may raise many doubts. S.K. has previously supported attention-getting techniques as making men aware; now he says abruptly:

> But everyone should keep silent insofar as he has no understanding to communicate. Merely to want to raise an outcry is a sort of glittering idleness.

This is somewhat startling, coming from a man who claimed he had no understanding to impart but who took as his Socratic task only to wake men up. S.K. had reserved teaching for God alone (cf. *The Fragments*), but now he wants the author who cannot instruct to keep silent. Once he claimed that exaggeration is the road to enlightenment; now he wants precision. Once he stressed the necessity for indirect communication; now he wants directness.

> . . . every premise author is devouring. He is devouring precisely because, instead of keeping silent, he utters doubts and makes an outcry.
>
> The art of all communication consists in coming as close as possible to reality, i.e., to contemporaries who are in the position of readers . . . (p. 9).

Passion had been Kierkegaard's password as the fault of the age. Now he adds a word of caution, perhaps after observing its excesses in Adler:

> It is one thing to depict a passionate man when with him is . . . a life view which can control him, and it is quite a different thing when a passionate man . . . becomes an author, runs amuck, and by the help of books assaults us as it were with his doubts and torments (p. 10).
>
> It is one thing to be a physician who knows all about cures and healing . . .—it is one thing to be a physician beside a sickbed, and another thing to be a sick man who leaps out of his bed by becoming an author, communicating bluntly the symptoms of his disease (p. 11)

Who is Kierkegaard writing about here? He claims that he wants to deal only with the written word and leave the author out of consideration. He finds he cannot do this with Adler, and yet he had made this impossible for us to avoid where he is concerned. S.K. complains of anyone who writes too hastily: "Nowadays one takes for a revelation any strong impression, and the same evening puts it in the newspaper" (p. 13). Kierkegaard claims only to be a serviceable critic, a lonely person, and warns us against confusing a genius with an apostolic existence.

Kierkegaard fears a growing sensuality, a dangerous temptation to cleverness in his time. Yet he claims to have no talent to write for "the instant." Oddly enough, this is the title he chose for his published attacks against the church. What he has written, he feels, applies to and can be read at all times. Seldom has S.K. spoken so loosely about the particular setting of the written analysis or divorced it so sharply from the individual and the circumstances.

Kierkegaard continues to upbraid Adler for changing his mind and announcing at a later time something different from what he once stated. (See footnote on p. 20.) And S.K. adds that one cannot treat the later saying as though it were the contemporaneous interpretation. This remark is interesting in view of the fact that S.K. changed his mind about himself as an author. He tells us in the *Point of View* that what he came to think in the end was actually what he had thought in the beginning. However, it certainly would not seem to be so if we believe his early writings when taken by themselves.

Adler is an "extraordinary" man, and Kierkegaard also certainly thought of himself as one, if not precisely in the same sense. Thus, it is interesting when S.K. dwells so long on the problem of "the extraordinary." Such a person can be the cause of the most frightful corruption, and he cannot render service to the Establishment by attacking its very life, S.K. now asserts. If such a man receives a revelation, fear and trembling appear as a result of any attempt to communicate it directly. Yet if such silence is maintained no authority can come from it. If God has called him to be an apostle, his silence only transforms this into the role of genius.

Divine authority is the decisive thing that makes one an apostle. Offense, which S.K. used to say came form the nonrationality of the concept of incarnation, he now sees as coming from the confrontation of genius with divine authority. Be he lowly or great, the offense is that a mere man possesses divine authority. We cannot, of course, always discern this at the time. ". . . Nowadays it is all too easy to understand that Peter was an apostle, but in those days people found it far easier to understand that he was a fisherman" (p. 25). The true apostle will not find it at all strange that many fail to recognize his authority. Only the genius who mistakes himself for an apostle will rant and rave over his lack of attention and use extreme means if necessary to bring attention to himself.

Yet Kierkegaard sees that a touch of genius must go with apostleship, to give the man the tools with which to translate his message. ". . . Paul too had a revelation; only that in addition he had an unusually good head" (p. 26). Whereas before questions have always been quite complex and agonizing for S.K., now suddenly at this point they become crystal clear: "The question is quite simple: Will you obey? Or will you not obey? Will you bow in faith before divine authority? Or will you be offended?"

S.K., who has engaged in infinitely subtle dialectic, now berates those who take refuge in the problems of exegesis or who treat the Scriptures so scientifically that they might as well be anonymous writings. Such tactics are merely evasive, he is convinced, and divert us from the real issue of obedience. Adler collided with the church because he clung to his individuality, and so did Kierkegaard. Strangely enough, in *The Book on Adler,* S.K. seems to be on the side of the church and its authority. The fundamental principles must be defended against reflection gone astray:

> And so it is with relation to the spiritual life, the most injurious thing when reflection, as it too often does, goes amiss and instead of being used for advantage brings the concealed labor of the hidden life out into the open and attacks the fundamental principles themselves (p. 30). But when the established order does not hold the reins tight, then finally every man who will not obey becomes a reformer (p. 33).

Consider all this as coming at a time when S.K. has just make public his pseudonymous authorship, has insisted on causing an uproar in the press, and is about to attack the established church himself. The most interesting people in the world certainly are of more than one mind about themselves! And in criticizing Adler, Kierkegaard sides with Bishop Mynster, whom he is shortly to attack on his deathbed. Here he has nothing but mild praise for the man. How quick and violent is the shift of an irrational mood to its opposite. Still,

S.K. asserts that a truly extraordinary individual is above any established order, but this is a dreadful responsibility if you have heard your call amiss. And you cannot complain about resistance from the established order, since the genuine apostle actually wants a suitable resistance. He needs firmness against which alone he can define himself. If everyone agrees with him, he is nothing extraordinary.

A truly extraordinary man is concerned with only his relationship to God. S.K. is sure that being victorious in the world is something he will be unconcerned about, a joking matter (pp. 40–41). "Conquering" is an inward affair, a matter of the spirit. Kierkegaard parodies worldly attempts to have things one's own way in one of his most graphic phrases:

> in case Jesus Christ did not conquer by being crucified, but had conquered in the modern style by business methods and a dreadful use of his talking gear . . . (p. 42, footnote).

Reflection and intelligence, the two marks of the modern age, are for the *extraordinarius* merely tools at his disposal. Profundity will not be in his words, in the utterance, in the statement, but will be only in his mode of existence (p. 48). Such a special individual will be a shock to the established order. However, the accomplishment of a divine task is necessarily slow, and one finds a remedy for the impatience of reflection only in faith, humility, and daily consecration (p. 50). Yet this labor goes on in silence: He who has a revelation has shut himself up within himself and keeps silent. Only his mode of life can betray him, not words.

When Kierkegaard moves on in Chapter II to consider the fact of revelation, he treats this as crucial for the modern age, which thinks of itself as historical. The Christian "fact" (the incarnation of God) has no history. It is not a part of historical study or sequence, since it stands immovably as a paradox. Faced with such a fact, time is of no importance. To have studied the matter for eighteen hundred years in itself brings one no closer to a solution than if the event happened yesterday (p. 63).

Thus it is that Adler becomes instructive. His appearance and his claim to revelation offer a contemporary example of what the Christian must always face. Adler's case removes the illusion of the aid which we expect from historical study by being an immediate event which demands decision without the benefit of historical study. Whether Adler himself is mistaken or not, his case offers a challenge to us all, since it confronts Christianity with a paradox in a contemporary setting. Without such cases, we are tempted to think of Christianity as an historical matter, whereas it is a contemporary affair. A case like Adler's reminds us of this fact.

"Adler is quite properly a sign" (p. 67). We must decided about him, whether he is God's elect or simply demonically shrewd. This is precisely the decision which must be put to any age, without the benefit of allowing men to treat it as a scholarly problem. More important than that, however, is the fact that an intellectual age confuses words *about* Christianity with the experience *of it.* When the formulae come alive in an individual who is already familiar with the doctrines, it produces a strange and baffling experience. In his haste, one is overcome by living through in fact what before he knew only as words. He looks about frantically for the strongest word he can find to describe his experience: "revelation." If we did not think of Christianity as a matter of knowledge, we would not get into this situation. Because we treat it as a matter of books and doctrines, Christian "experience" comes over us in a strange-but-yet-known way. Then we reach for extra-ordinary categories to describe it. The experience has made the already known words weak by comparison, and they no longer seem adequate.

S.K. goes on to analyze Adler's claim to revelation in Chapter III. What he cannot abide is the conceit involved in Adler's publishing his experiences and the tumult with which Adler surrounds it. An enthusiast, a religiously awakened man he may be, but the problem comes in over-stepping the bounds of privacy. In creating a public fuss he claims more, and in this way calls attention to the individual, rather than to the experience itself or to Christianity. To be moved quite dramatically and personally needs to be distinguished from a claim to a new revelation of doctrine. Yet the personal force of the experience tends to obscure this line, as S.K.'s "Easter experience" perhaps did for him. ". . . There is a decisive qualitative difference between being rescued in a miraculous way, and being entrusted by revelation with a new doctrine" (p. 86).

Up until now Kierkegaard has been trying to draw some important distinctions: the qualitative line between genius and an apostle,
the words of Christianity vs. the experience of it, a personally miraculous experience vs. a new doctrine revealed, a private experience vs.
a public communication. As important as all this is for Kierkegaard
as well as for Adler, he never excludes the possibility of new doctrines
being privately revealed. He draws crucial distinctions, but he does
not rule out any individual case or set any one objective standard—
that is, until he comes to the end of the first section: "It is true that
Christianity is built upon a revelation, but also it is limited by the
definite revelation it has received" (p. 92). These are important words
coming from a man who has stressed Christianity's subjective existence and its subjective appropriation. Now he claims a definite norm
to which all experiences must conform and by which each may be
tested.

Whatever Adler's personal situation or conviction, his views can
and should be judged by an external criterion. S.K. goes on to pronounce him a "confused genius." Evidently, Kierkegaard now finds
a clear and objective standard which can be referred to and by which
the inner tortures of a struggling religious passion may ultimately be
judged. Passion, inwardness, and subjectivity have been S.K.'s key
words up until now. These are not set aside, and none of Kierkegaard's interest in the personal struggle over religion is diminished.
As he develops his criterion with Adler, it is interesting to see that,
when all the inner struggle is over, its fruits may then be judged by
some already established norm. In fact, they must be. However creative and subtle the person, Christianity knows only one original revelation, and all later works are subjected to its rule.

A sidelight to be sure, but still an interesting sidelight, is S.K.'s
strong objection to Adler for having published too many books in one
year. The parallel in circumstances to Kierkegaard's own fantastic
publication rate is quite amusing, and it is easy to see why S.K. is so
sensitive on this point. S.K. does not overlook this fact, and he seems
to think he has a way of protecting himself from this same criticism.
The reasons are rather minute, and the reader is advised to "judge for
yourself" whether S.K.'s excuses are valid or sophistical. His objec-
tions against excessive length are particularly humorous in view of

Kierkegaard's own doctrine of "repetition" and his own excessive use of words (pp. 94–97).

Among the various writers in Christendom, how is one to distinguish the genius from the apostle? Kierkegaard has often discussed genius, and he clearly considers himself an equal to any in those ranks. He said that it was "reflection" he had to oppose in his day, and he felt that it took intellectual powers equal to the finest to do this. As time goes on, he increasingly stresses the religious. He becomes more convinced of the essential rightness of his own approach and the essential wrongness of other current views of Christianity.

This being the case, S.K. is bound to think more and more about the signs of genuine discipleship, although previously he disclaimed authority for himself completely. Then along comes Adler, openly claiming what Kierkegaard had heretofore said must be held in secret. All the while S.K. had been gaining momentum toward revealing himself directly. Kierkegaard had stressed inwardness and indirection. Adler is direct and outer just at a time when S.K. is tending in this direction himself.

Kierkegaard has prided himself on the poetic quality of his writing. Now he declares that Paul, the model apostle, ranks rather low as a stylist (p. 105). Plato and Socrates had often been S.K.'s models. They even provide the basis for his analysis of Christianity in the *Fragments.* Now Plato is put in another class and ruled qualitatively distinct from the genuine apostle. The genius is what he is by reason of himself. S.K.'s pride in his own authorship has been obvious, but an apostle is what he is by reason of his divine authority. A genius can straighten out his early paradoxes, just as S.K. comes to see his authorship clearly in his last years. But an apostle is a man called and sent by God, one not really dissimilar from S.K.'s earlier analysis of Abraham. Aesthetic grounds allow us to appraise the genius; divine authority is the only decisive factor for the apostle. In his writing S.K. has basked in his own cleverness, but now he sees clearly that one obeys Paul only because he has divine authority, whether or not Paul is clever. Kierkegaard has drawn this distinction many times before, but seldom has he rested the religious claim on God's authority.

Christianity's current confusion comes from its uncertainty about God. This leads, in the ensuing rebellion, to a forgetfulness about

what divine authority is. In his earlier writings, S.K. had had diag-
nosed Christianity as lacking inwardness and passion. Now the confusion of our age is said to come, not from superficiality, but from a
failure to submit (p. 108). Doubt is now the culprit. Yet it is S.K. who
has given us the definitive analysis that made excruciating doubt into
a necessary prerequisite to faith. Doubt degrades God, Kierkegaard
now says. It pulls him down to ordinary levels, whereas what he needs
is to be above doubt. Instead of obeying, men engage in cross-exami-
nation, and here the criteria tend to be cleverness and profundity.

At this point S.K. reaches a climax in his argument. Listen and
see if, when taken on its own, it does not sound for all the world like
Karl Barth:

> Authority . . . is something which remains unchanged, which
> one cannot acquire by having understood the doctrine in the
> fullest sense. Authority is a specific quality which comes from
> another place and makes itself felt precisely when the content
> of the saying or of the action is assumed to be indifferent (p.
> 110).

Kierkegaard goes on to say that to preach is to exercise authority.
What preaching means is the enunciation of what the age has forgotten. If he sees this as the prerequisite for preaching, and if he denies
authority for himself, this perhaps kept S.K. from leaving all else to
go and preach. The religious revolution within Kierkegaard leads him
away from the ministry rather than to it, as it does for so many who
discover its divine demands. Before, he had found the demands of
religion all to be inner; now they require an external authority given
to the individual. It is often said that Barth rebelled against an early
existentialism. It is interesting to speculate as to whether he might
have learned his rebellion from Kierkegaard, just as S.K. may have
learned it from Adler.

Kierkegaard now stresses an external, essential, qualitative difference between God and man. The qualification, "an apostle," belongs
in the sphere of transcendence (p. 112), a sphere S.K. has not heretofore said much about. He treats profundity casually, too. The profound has characterized all of systematic theology. It entices men as
if it could make them believe, but this is confusing. Doubt has been
a part of all existential thought, but now S.K. says that doubt merely

makes men embarrassed to obey, and thus it essentially works against Christianity, not for it.

It is an affectation to want to believe in Christianity on account of profundity. This is S.K.'s new line, and according to him all of modern speculation is "affected." It has done away with obedience and authority but still wants to believe orthodoxy. Genius projects itself and is active in the world. It accomplishes perhaps more than ten businessmen, but there is nothing about this work which is transcendent. The genius lives withdrawn from the world in self-satisfaction (p. 121). The man called by revelation has become an instrument of God, to go out into the world, to labor, and to suffer. It is precisely here that S.K. rants against the clever writer, one who is at ease in his study publishing collections of his cleverness. What could be a more devastating criticism of S.K.'s own career?

For simple men silence is the expression of inwardness. But S.K. now demands "connection and continuity" in expression (p. 124). He pronounces Adler to be "deranged" because his writings lack these qualities, and yet it is Kierkegaard who has ruled a "system" out as being now impossible. Before S.K. has always lauded genius; now he qualifies this praise by asserting that dizziness is the essential character of genius, propounding dizzy aesthetic views. ". . . Dizziness results when the eye has no fixed point on which to rest" (p. 127). The remedy for this is spiritual discipline and limitation. Contrast all this with S.K.'s usual characterization of the believer as one suspended over 70,000 fathoms of water. Kierkegaard evidently now feels that philosophy only confuses the religious life (p. 145), whereas before Socrates had served as his model in the *Fragments.* Yet a decisive change, such as Adler's conversion away from Hegel, should not be given immediate outer expression, S.K. is convinced. Kierkegaard now recommends a slow outer reflection.

In the last chapter Kierkegaard begins to return to his early theme of inwardness as the essential mark of religiousness. He pauses to observe a somewhat similar stylistic effect in his own writings and in Adler's. But then he moves on to a crucial distinction:

> to be shaken . . . is the more universal foundation for all religiousness; the experience of being shaken, of being deeply moved, the coming into being of subjectivity in the inwardness

of emotion, the pious pagan and the pious Jew have in common with the Christian. And one does not become a Christian by being moved by something indefinitely higher, and not every outpouring of religious emotion is a Christian outpouring (p. 163).

Specifically Christian concepts have been defined by a revelation given once and for all. Thus, to qualify as a Christian, such a passionate experience must be more that profoundly inward. It must fit defined Christian categories. One can acquire skill and schooling in Christian concepts, S.K. is now convinced. An awakening is required, yes, but so are conceptual and terminological firmness and definiteness (p. 165).

All this has an interesting similarity to the famous disctinction S.K. outlines near the end of the *Postscript* between Religiousness A and Religiousness B. Religiousness A is general; Religiousness B is specifically Christian. But a careful examination reveals that his distinction in *Authority and Revelation* is even more clear-cut. Now it is objectively oriented and non-dialectical. Perhaps it is Adler, who was on Kierkegaard's mind at the writing of the *Postscript,* who induced him to make this crucial distinction. Perhaps in thinking directly about Adler, it comes home to S.K. with even greater clarity, for now he accuses Adler of confining religion to subjectivity. ". . . He confounds the subjective with the objective, his subjectively altered condition with an external event . . ." (p. 168). The famous originator of the view that "objectively Christianity has no existence" *(Postscript)* now says something quite different.

Every believer must be conscious that religion has not arisen in his heart, that Christianity has an objective determinant.

> Christianity exists before any Christian exists, it must exist in order that one may become a Christian, it contains the determinant by which one may test whether one has become a Christian, it maintains its objective subsistence apart from all believers, while at the same time it is the inwardness of the believer (p. 168).

S.K. has not abandoned inwardness as a condition, just as he never overlooked the existence of objective doctrine in the earlier *Postscript.* Now, however, the solidity of Christianity's objective existence is clearly stressed, and the objective and subjective sides are brought into more equal proportions. Again, there is little in the statement above which Barth could not endorse. Thus, we might say that Barth developed the late Kierkegaardian "right," and Paul Tillich has held on to the gloomy Dane's "leftish" view while still attempting a systematization.

Now S.K. recommends that one remain silent about any inner change. The one affected should act and labor rather than be productive in a literary way (p. 170). This certainly is not what S.K. did himself. Rather than subjectivity, Kierkegaard concludes with a rather startling phrase: "the point of departure is from above, from God" (p. 192). And in summarizing Adler he seems prophetic about his own excesses soon to come and the violation of his own restrictions: ". . . as a pagan he became a Christian priest, and that when he had undeniably come somewhat closer to being a Christian he was deposed" (p. 178).

All of S.K.'s early energy is devoted to the problem of becoming a Christian. Now he discovers in Adler a startling clarity that, if too much energy is sent inward, the violence of this propulsion may, ironically, not only send one to the mark but far beyond it. Did S.K. heed his own advice and remain content to stop with faith, or did the violence of his inner subjectivity, when made public, also propel him way out beyond it?

III
Passion vs. Submission

Some reference has already been made to Kierkegaard's other doctrines and writings. But if we are to understand S.K. from the "point of view" of *Authority and Revelation,* a brief review and comparison with his complete writings is in order. Let us proceed in rough chronological sequence. This will also provide an overall context within which the reader can then study his major concepts and categories.

The Journals (trans. A. Dru, Harper Torchbook Edition, 1959) cover the whole period of his authorship, but not his whole life. In the strictest sense they are intellectual journals. They are not comments on people and places and events, but commentaries on religious and intellectual concerns from a personal perspective. Although S.K. tells us that he had no expectation of leading a happy earthly life, that he was torn asunder inwardly (p. 40), all this must be contrasted with the outer stability in which he lived comfortably, cared for by servants and secretaries.

It is in the *Journals* that he complains about the lack of passion in the age (p. 77), and he denies that after his death anyone will be able to find the final words that will explain everything (p. 85). In Adler perhaps S.K. saw a startling example of passion without external restraints. If we can apply established categories, perhaps more can be explained than when just the inner life is considered. He talks of silence, of becoming a priest, of not making himself intelligible to anyone, of his ideal to live for marriage.

All this comes just at the moment when he is about to settle himself in the opposite of these intentions. He is aware of a metamorphosis, and it comes at the time he is writing about Adler and struggles through numerous revisions and prefaces. Perhaps it is Adler who made Kierkegaard aware of himself and made him determined to speak out, as Adler had done and for which Kierkegaard had criticized him. Then in an entry in 1849 (p. 153) Kierkegaard explains the strange discrepancy between his written words and the facts of his life:

> What does being a poet mean? It means having one's own personal life in quite different categories from those of one's poetic work, it means being related to the ideal in imagination only, so that one's own personal life is more or less a satire on poetry and on oneself.

Yet Adler lived what he proclaimed and spoke directly. Is it he who moved Kierkegaard to forget indirection and in his last days to forsake the role of the poet for that of the martyr?

Either/Or (trans. David Swenson, Oxford Univ. Press, 1946) is S.K.'s first book, but because of the fuss he created in his later life, it tends to be either forgotten or countermanded. It is here that Kierkegaard meditates upon any external mode of life that exists in complete contradiction to an inner life (p. 4). But after the Adler affair he will spend time trying to prove that this was not the case in his own life. In his introduction to *Either/Or,* S.K. perhaps gives the best clue both to it and to himself. These two radically opposed views of life, the aesthetic and the ethical, might be the work of one man he suggests (p. 11). If so, one need not try to straighten everything out in life in order to put it on a single plane. Life is never finished; it simply ends, and no one standpoint can ever explain it. We only know that one person was capable of living in several ways.

In the late pages of Volume II (p. 200), S.K. says that the tears a man sheds for himself bear no fruit, but to feel oneself guilty and to cry in repentance is a genuine act. The second volume closes with what is essentially a sermon on S.K.'s favorite theme, "against God we are always wrong." It is impossible not to note that he sheds many tears for himself in his life's closing days. Instead of ending on a note of guilt and wrongness before God, ironically he ends his days by asserting his absolute rightness. In this case the earlier ending seems more profound than the later and actual finale.

The Edifying Discourses (trans. D. Swenson, Harper Torchbook Edition, ed. Paul Holmer, 1958), yield perhaps the best insight when placed next to *Authority and Revelation.* Kierkegaard insists that these are discourses, not sermons, because he has no authority to preach (p. 1). The concept of "authority" does not appear earlier in his writings; it is only in these unpreached sermons which are essentially devotional meditations. To one familiar with the Kierkegaard of *Fear and Trembling,* a first reading of any *Discourse* may come as a shock. Here there is no anxiety, no tension, no strain or shouting. These are meditations, and the author both seems to know God and to be calm in his relationship to him.

Not to say but to do has often been his theme (p. 67), just as the rarest kind of greatness is often described as the person who knows that of himself he can do absolutely nothing (p. 151). Kierkegaard sees that inwardly no outer circumstance can be essential. Internally man strives only against himself (p. 166) and thus ought to attack no one else. When compared with *Authority and Revelation* and his more vociferous "dialectical" writings, this question arises: *If these works reveal two such different Kierkegaards in his views on the nature of the religious life, could it be that the experience with Adler broke the wall which separated the calmness of the devotional works from the storm of the "dialectical" writings?* Calmness and clarity was always present before, but only in an isolated devotional sphere. Now it becomes the standard for all of the religious life and also for technical theology.

Perhaps Adler's excesses taught S.K. the need for external norms within which to contain the stress and strain of inward struggle. The lesson Kierkegaard learned was the necessity of bringing these two sides of the religious life together. In Adler S.K. saw his own earlier extreme subjectivity detached from the theological tradition, as it never actually had been with Kierkegaard. The *Discourses* reveal a man who is very sure of God within traditional Christian formulations. S.K. did not go to Adler's brink of heresy. But he saw how far astray independent subjectivity could go—even to madness. He recoiled in order to bring the inner religious life back under *Authority and Revelation.*

Repetition (trans. W. Lowrie, Princeton Univ. Press, 1946) is one of Kierkegaard's most fascinating little books. Because he claims that originally it was "misunderstood," in the preface he writes some of his most insightful comments on authorship, already quoted. If we consider his later direct outbursts and his criticism of Adler's quick announcements, his views on irony and silence are most illuminating:

> He did not have the strength to carry out the plan. His soul lacked the elasticity of irony. He had not the strength to take irony's vow of silence, not the power to keep it; and only the man who keeps silent amounts to anything (p. 27).

Was Kierkegaard mistaken? Did he forget his earlier advice when he decided in his last days to speak out and to do so with violence? Did he carry this view forward to apply it to Adler in judgment only to be unable to restrain himself? Kierkegaard stressed man's frail humanity. It is all too human to be unable to heed one's own advice and to discern one's own flaws most clearly in others.

With *Fear and Trembling,* (trans. W. Lowrie, Princeton Univ. Press, 1945) one of S.K.'s most interesting comparisons emerges: Abraham and Adler. Like Abraham, Adler thought he was acting on direct divine instruction. The individual is higher than the universal, and this involves a suspension of normal modes of judgment. With Adler, Kierkegaard wants to find a norm against which his excesses may be measured, and S.K. finds that the original Christian revelation provides a check. On the other hand, S.K. is more radical in interpreting Abraham. He defines faith as beginning where thinking leaves off, and he advises his age to stop with faith. "Faith is this paradox, and the individual absolutely cannot make himself intelligible to anyone" (p. 115). Only the individual can decide. No one outside can decide whether he is a knight of faith or is in temptation, since religion is inwardness which is incommensurable with the outer (p. 120), a subjectivity incommensurable with reality. We can allow such a radical interpretation of faith to stand with Abraham because he maintains himself within the tradition. But Adler stepped outside, and Kierkegaard suddenly saw the necessity to establish limits. Yet to do so requires changing his doctrine of the radical subjectivity of faith. So Adler taught S.K. something which Abraham could not do.

In the *Philosophical Fragments* (trans. D. Swenson, Princeton Univ. Press, 1962) Kierkegaard actually does mention the concept of authority; but, interestingly enough, he does so only to deny that any human being can ever truly be an authority for another (p. 7). Error is something only the individual can discover for himself alone (p. 9). And in the case of Christianity, it cannot be checked by knowledge, since "no knowledge can have for its object the absurdity that the eternal is the historical" (p. 50). ". . . Belief is not a form of knowledge, but a free act, an expression of will" (p. 68). Rational tests for faith seem impossible, since Christianity's core is an unassimilatable paradox that exists as an object for faith alone (p. 80).

If S.K. had applied this standard to Adler, he could not have denied him his position. Yet, Kierkegaard knew that Adler's views were the product of a deranged mind and thus must be rejected. He introduces the authority of the original divine revelation, and essentially it is God who provides the ground for judgment. The seed of this doctrine is, in fact, present in the *Fragments,* but men are not allowed to assume the divine standpoint for purposes of judging the faith of another man. However, Adler went too far, and God's point of view had to be introduced as a check, although it is now wielded by man.

In The *Concept of Dread* (trans. Lowrie, 1946) Kierkegaard considers the "religious genius." The topic is interesting in itself, since much of *Authority and Revelation* is based upon a radical distinction between the two. In the earlier work S.K. describes him, this religious genius: "The first thing he does is to turn towards himself. For by the fact that he turns toward himself he turns *eo ipso* towards God . . ." (p. 96). This of course fits Kierkegaard's early equation of the subjective and the religious, but Adler's subjectivity actually carried him away from God. So S.K. ended by establishing objective norms and denying that the genius could *per se* be called religious.

The Concluding Unscientific Postscript (trans. Swenson and Lowrie, Princeton Univ. Press, 1944) was intended to complete S.K.'s published works, but as he finished it he changed his mind. This switch is interesting in relation to Adler, since its almost constant theme is "subjectivity," and we know that Adler was on S.K.'s mind at the same time. "God exists only for subjectivity in inwardness" (p. 178). The conformity of thought and being is actually realized only in God, so that no existing individual in the process of becoming can judge with authority. What happens to alter this important doctrine? Is S.K. assuming the role of God in his later writings? In the devotional works S.K. had known God with calmness and clarity, so that Adler's subjectivity may have frightened Kierkegaard into introducing the traditional theological perspective. Heretofore, S.K. had stressed the human, subjective mode.

If taken literally the *Postscript* provides no standard by which we can test Adler's demented doctrines. For the *Postscript,* to believe against the understanding is martyrdom, so that Adler would appear to be a martyr. Reading S.K.'s early radical subjectivity, it is easy to see why Adler should have thought he would find a defender in Kierkegaard when he came to him to plead for support. It is equally easy to see why S.K., when faced with Adler, should have found the experience unsettling. Inwardness cannot be directly communicated, and indirect communication is the only true way (p. 246), Kierkegaard has said. Yet there stands Adler who must be dealt with directly and objectively ruled out of bounds. Christianity is said no to be a doctrine (p. 339), and yet Adler is crazy and subjective and not within the bounds of doctrine. A sane man who actually stays within traditional bounds (as S.K. did) can be allowed to espouse radical doctrines. However, a crazy man cannot be allowed to be a radical, and so Adler forces a change upon Kierkegaard. In the *Postscript* S.K. denies external authority; in *Authority and Revelation* it becomes a needed concept.

In *The Point of View* (trans. W. Lowrie, Oxford Univ. Press, 1939) Kierkegaard discusses his relation to all of his works, which he had said in the appendix to the *Postscript* he could not do. There he told us that he could never claim the pseudonymous works as his own, since their anonymity prevents anyone from claiming a personal relationship to words which were so written. Having made the claim that no word can be uttered in his own name, he ends the *Postscript* with a plea: "And, oh, that no half-hearted man would lay a dialectical hand upon this work, but would let it stand as it now stands!" (Feb., 1846). His *Journal* records his intention at this time to give up being an author and prepare himself to be a pastor. As fate would have it, however, it is Kierkegaard himself hardly two years later in the *Point of View* who will not let the *Postscript* stand. He insists on claiming all his pseudonymous works personally, and he violates his norm of indirect communication with a sometimes violent direct discourse. Why? Although Kierkegaard did not intend to reveal himself by writing about Adler, is his indirect communication still better, as the early S.K. would believe, than his own later direct summary?

In *The Point of View* S.K.'s psychological concepts are ignored. They are not accounted for in his self-appraisal, and many times before S.K. has claimed to be only a psychologist. So *The Point of View* cannot explain all of the authorship. Without recounting the various explanations of *The Point of View,* it is enough to see that they run counter to all that S.K. has said about communication heretofore. Of course, *The Point of View* is not all of a piece. In moments of lucidity S.K. seems to realized the impossibility of what he is trying to do in explaining his authorship so bluntly and overtly. When he does, he returns again to his themes of duplicity from first to last, the maintenance of ambiguity that makes a final explanation impossible, and that a desire to prevent all misunderstanding is a sign of youth not maturity.

What drove S.K. to these personal and verbal extremes in his late years? Few if any took Adler's doctrines seriously, and in that sense he could not have been a threat to Kierkegaard. Yet S.K. reacts like a man who has been challenged to the core. It was he who challenged *The Corsair,* not *vice versa,* and it was he who attacked a dead bishop who could not return the challenge. But Adler was alive and crazy, and yet he may have been the one who gave Kierkegaard's radical doctrines their most decisive challenge. Subjectively Adler conformed to them while being objectively deranged.

IV
God vs. Man

Kierkegaard continues to write his *Edifying Discourses* from first to last in his career. *Training in Christianity* (trans. W. Lowrie, Princeton Univ. Press, 1941) comes late in his life and thus may have some special significance. The self-induced outer storm is on. Yet in this work his religious life is still quiet and, if anything, deeper. A contrite heart and a consciousness of sin are the narrow way into the Christianity he outlines. In the public press, however, S.K. is at the same time talking of popular persecution and protesting his own ultimate rightness. The *Two Discourses* (in *For Self-Examination,* trans. W. Lowrie, Princeton Univ. Press, 1944) come in 1851, well after S.K.'s Easter experience that his sins were not only forgiven but "forgotten." In these discourses he gives an entirely different account of how a Christian authorship should end. This is so radically different from the events of his last years, which ended in a near riot at his funeral, that it is hard to compare. Yet it is so significant that a word from his *Discourses* should not be overlooked as a contrasting summary:

> A gradually progressing work as a writer which had its beginning in *Either/Or* seeks here its definite point of rest at the foot of the altar, where the author, who personally knows best his imperfection and guilt, does not by any means call himself a witness for the truth, but only a peculiar sort of poet and thinker who, "without authority," has nothing new to bring (p. 4).

The quietness, the inwardness, the return to his self-description as a poet and thinker—all this is striking after the violence of his claim to religious authorship only a few years before in *The Point of View.* Yet like *The Book on Adler, The Point of View* was never published in S.K.'s lifetime. It is possible that Kierkegaard himself could never quite bring the two works, and the causes which induced them, into clear focus. The ending he gives for his authorship as quoted above is so startlingly in contrast to the strong words of his last years that it is hard to accept. Yet perhaps the uncontrolled violence and extremes of the last years gave S.K. an insight into himself. His words and not his deeds, as befits a poet, are to be accepted as his truest record.

S.K. has denied that he can be a witness to the truth. Yet in reading *Attack Upon Christendom* (trans. W. Lowrie, Princeton Univ. Press, 1946), it is hard to hear the strong words there without the distinct impression that Kierkegaard at least at times fancied himself as a "witness." In the first place, he now speaks out in direct judgment, whereas before he has used indirection as the modest method befitting a mere poet. As he begins to define a "genuine witness," it is hard to think that he does not have himself partly in mind.

A witness must be unacquainted with enjoyment and initiated into suffering. S.K. tells us time and time again that this applies to him, and yet it does not appear outwardly to be true. A witness must live in poverty and abasement, unappreciated, derided, etc. S.K. spent his fortune and lived well while it lasted. In his religious writings he would abase himself, but he did not do so in his poetic authorship. In his later years he even worked to bring insults upon himself. Kierkegaard says that his only task is the Socratic task (p. 283), to revise the definition of Christianity and to prove that others fit it even less than he. But if Christianity is inwardness and subjectivity, he cannot tell from any outward sign whether the good Bishop or anyone else is or is not the genuine article. Adler has forced him to set out more overt definitions, but the result of this seems to create a violent public outburst.

Kierkegaard is a puzzle to his biographers and to theologians because there are so many of him. If such decisive and drastic changes had not taken place in his later years, appraisal might be easier. But, when he acts against his earlier advice and changes so radically, when he switches to claim that his own interpretations are the truth, all is reduced to chaos. If Adler at least helped to induce this reaction, one thing we see in the later writings is an over-compensation for the

shortcomings in the early doctrines. These extravagances were made vividly clear to S.K. in a startling case history. Adler fits S.K.'s example too well and yet he is deranged.

In turning away from Adler, Kierkegaard perhaps turned too far too fast, as fits his own description of life. In a crazy example he may have been brought closer to the truth than in the subtle dialectic, a conclusion with which at least a majority of our many Kierkegaards might agree. After all, in Christian doctrine it ought not to be so shocking if one's crucial lessons are learned through strange people —even a deranged minister or a self-centered philosopher.

Does all this make a "system" out of Kierkegaard's writings? Hardly. There are too many built-in impediments for that. Just when one thinks he has an answer, another statement takes it away. In between the tedious lines, the romantic exaggeration and self-absorption, there is many an instructive phrase which any individual reader can find. Kierkegaard formally may have changed his mind and his method. Yet in doing so, in the long run he was more consistent with his deeper insights than if he had continued on the same theme, or not upset the apple cart by resuming his authorship on a new vein.

Perhaps S.K. was strong and clever enough to keep the weakness in his own views covered—from himself as well as from others. When he saw them defenselessly exposed in another, he was unstrung. Kierkegaard was radical in his subjectivity, but objectively he never moved away from orthodoxy. Considering Adler's defiant self-confidence in his own wild views, S.K. brought the clear, calm objectivity, which had always been a part of his devotional literature, together with the necessity for subjectivity and inwardness in the genuine religious life. But this clue came too late, and S.K. did not see how the lessons learned in Adler might apply to him.

In the early writing and through the *Postscript,* he is clearly the man who struggles with God by struggling with himself. In the devotional writings, and finally in *Authority and Revelation,* it is God once again who seems to have man on his terms. However, S.K. could not let it stand that way in his own last public years. Instead he asserted himself more blatantly than he ever had before. As Kierkegaard says of Abraham, however, a man is great in proportion to the greatest of that with which he strove, and he who struggles with God becomes the greatest of all. The struggle of God vs. man is the classic religious theme, and certainly it permeates Kierkegaard's life.

It is just that he should have ended, to borrow one of his curtain speeches, by being brought to rest at the foot of the altar prepared to confess his guilt. Instead, he ends shaking his fist at the world and announcing that God has certified his rightness. All he forgot was one of his favorite sermon themes: As Against God We Are Always in the Wrong, with which he closed his earliest large book, *Either/Or.* Had he done this, he might have ended exactly where he began, a very nice Kierkegaardian thing to do. However, like any reader of his, S.K. certainly ends by being more edified by all that he has forced himself to go through.